KU-549-165

Preface

This report has been produced as part of a project funded by the Joseph Rowntree Foundation and we thank the Foundation for its support. We are grateful to Andrew Dilnot, who has read numerous drafts and given invaluable advice. Thanks are also due to Howard Reed and to participants at a seminar at the Institute for Fiscal Studies. Any remaining errors are entirely our own.

Data from the Family Resources Survey and the Family Expenditure Survey were kindly supplied by the Department of Social Security.

The views expressed in this report are those of the authors and not of the Joseph Rowntree Foundation nor of the Institute for Fiscal Studies, which has no corporate views.

Tom Clark is a Research Economist at IFS.

Christopher Giles is economics reporter at the BBC. For much of the period of research on this project, he was a Programme Co-ordinator at IFS.

John Hall is a Senior Research Economist at IFS. He is currently on secondment at the Department for the Environment, Transport and the Regions.

Does Council Tax Benefit Work?

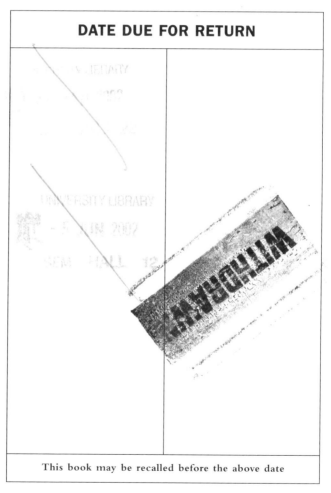

Published by
The Institute for Fiscal Studies
7 Ridgmount Street
London WC1E 7AE
tel. (44) 171 291 4800
fax (44) 171 323 4780
email: mailbox@ifs.org.uk
internet: http//www.ifs.org.uk

Printed by Bell and Bain Ltd, Glasgow

Contents

Executive summary   vii

1   Council tax and council tax benefit   1
   1.1   Background to the council tax   2
   1.2   The council tax   3
   1.3   Variation of council tax across households   8
   1.4   Council tax benefit   10

2   The distributional impact of council tax benefit   13
   2.1   Methods and data   14
   2.2   Council tax benefit and the income distribution   16
   2.3   Does council tax benefit fail the poorest households?   18
   2.4   Households that do not claim their council tax benefit   24
   2.5   Who gets council tax benefit?   27
   2.6   Conclusions   37

3   Changes over time   38
   3.1   Evolution of council tax rates since 1993   38
   3.2   Regional impact of council tax rises   42
   3.3   Distributional impact of rising council tax bills   46
   3.4   Conclusions   48

4   Reforms to council tax benefit   50
    4.1   Reform 1: increase income support rates   52
    4.2   Reform 2: exempt vulnerable groups   59
    4.3   Reform 3: replace council tax benefit with a   62
            'circuit breaker'
    4.4   Reform 4: abolish second-adult rebate   66
    4.5   Reform 5: abolish non-dependant deductions   67
    4.6   Reform 6: restrict council tax benefit to a   68
            band B bill
    4.7   Reform 7: pay council tax benefit as if all   70
            councils spent at SSA
    4.8   Reform 8: reduce council tax bills   72
    4.9   Reform 9: change band relativities   74

5   Conclusions: the policy agenda   77

    Appendix A   The council tax benefit system   80
    Appendix B   Comparing the FRS data with   84
                          administrative data from the DSS

    References   87

Executive Summary

Reform of the Welfare State is central to the government's agenda. Major reforms of benefits for pensioners, disabled people and the working poor have already been put in train. Yet council tax benefit, which is received by more people than any other means-tested benefit, has largely been overlooked in discussions of reform. But spending on it has increased in real terms every year since it was introduced and there is evidence of large-scale non-take-up. This report asks whether council tax benefit has a role to play in the contemporary Welfare State, and whether it can be made to work better.

The council tax is the only tax in the UK fiscal system to have its own means-tested benefit. This is because, like most property-based taxes, council tax is regressive — it represents a higher proportion of income for poorer households than for the rich. Its regressivity and local variability could combine to undermine the notion of a national 'safety net' — a minimum income below which society does not want any family to fall. Council tax benefit's primary role is to rescue this safety net by ensuring that low-income households receive compensation for council tax. It awards means-tested assistance to individuals and families up to a maximum of their total council tax liability.

In principle, the rules of council tax benefit are well designed to help those in most need. We find that council tax benefit sharply reduces the council tax liability of many poorer households that would otherwise face very high burdens from the tax. Help is successfully targeted at lone parents, those living in social housing and the unemployed, amongst others.

Nevertheless, there are some major problems with how council tax benefit works in practice. The benefit system leaves relatively high burdens on those in the middle of the income distribution, who are overwhelmingly without entitlement, and it also leaves pensioners facing a high burden from the tax. It breaks the link between local spending decisions and the council tax that households actually pay. Most importantly, it is highly complex, which makes the processing of claims time-consuming and costly and discourages take-up. Low take-up is a particular concern because the benefit needs to be judged according to whether it actually delivers to the needy, not just on how it targets entitlement. The cleverly designed rules of council tax benefit aim to protect the safety net, but low levels of take-up threaten the achievement of this aim. We examine a number of reforms that attempt to address the various problems.

Taken in isolation, complete abolition of council tax benefit cannot be squared with the maintenance of an income safety net. It would simplify the benefit system dramatically, but at the cost of hitting the poorest households in high-tax areas. Even if some simplicity were forgone and other benefits were modified in an attempt to replicate the workings of council tax benefit, significant numbers of the genuinely needy would be likely to lose out. The simple fact is that the council tax is sufficiently regressive and at sufficiently high rates to mean that it contributes importantly to the low incomes of many poorer households. It follows that the council tax bill that a family faces is an important factor in determining how well off we judge it to be. If the benefit system is to target help where it is needed most, it must therefore take council tax bills into account, in just the same way that incomes of family members, numbers of children and rents need to be taken into account, even though the inevitable upshot is a complex benefit system.

We also consider a number of less radical reforms, which assume the continuation of some form of local tax relief. Replacing means testing with simple exemptions for 'vulnerable groups' such as pensioners, as is common overseas, would considerably simplify administration. But council tax benefit is more effectively targeted than these systems. Replacing means testing with exemptions for broad, vulnerable groups gives help to many who are not poor and who do not receive help under the current system. So either some low-income groups would have to lose out or overall expenditure would have to rise. American-style systems, which limit the share of income that any household can be asked to pay in local tax, would involve even more means testing and would benefit those on middle incomes at the expense of the poorest households.

The easiest reforms to implement would be those that merely modify the present structure of council tax benefit. One possibility is abolishing the system's complex add-ons — single-adult rebates and non-dependant deductions. This reform would considerably simplify the council tax benefit means test but would affect the underlying fairness of the council tax and may influence house-sharing incentives. The questionable benefits of the minor simplification achieved might not justify the costs of further upheaval of the benefit system. Restricting the extent to which benefit payment adjusts to match council tax bills would offer a possible means of increasing the responsibility of recipients for the value of their property or the spending decision of their council. But such reform would compromise the targeting of the current system without offering much in the way of simplification, and it would also necessitate collecting local tax revenue from the poorest — a process that proved very inefficient under the community charge.

If a combination of lower council tax rates and higher levels of means-tested benefits were ever to prevail, then the abolition of council tax benefit would become much more attractive, principally because of the simplification it would represent. But in the short term, high (and upward-trended) tax rates mean that very steep increases in other means-tested benefits would be required to ensure that the abolition of local tax relief did not throw many of those facing high bills into poverty.

CHAPTER 1
Council Tax and Council Tax Benefit

The cost of council tax benefit has risen in real terms each year since its introduction in April 1993, despite falling unemployment which would normally be expected to reduce the number of claimants of means-tested benefits. Its structure is complex and contributes to the concern that the benefit system is failing to 'make work pay'. This report examines the structure and workings of council tax benefit and examines the options for reform.

The remainder of this chapter describes how council tax and council tax benefit operate, enabling us to explain and to evaluate critically the rationale for a specific system of relief for the council tax.

Chapter 2 uses evidence from the Family Resources Survey to assess how council tax benefit modifies the burden of the council tax across the income distribution. We identify where in the income distribution council tax has the heaviest impact and which types of household are affected. Chapter 3 charts how the burden of council tax has changed over time and draws out the implications of these changes for the benefit system.

Chapter 4 considers a number of options for reform. These range from the most radical, involving the complete abolition of local tax relief, to more incremental reforms that work within the existing structure of the benefit to solve particular problems. Chapter 5 concludes, weighing the strength of the argument for radical reform against the merits of the current system.

1.1. Background to the Council Tax

The council tax and council tax benefit came into force in Great Britain[1] in April 1993, marking the end of a period of considerable turmoil in local government finance. Its immediate predecessor, the community charge or 'poll tax', became unworkable as widespread resentment against the 'unfairness' of the tax was associated with non-compliance on a scale rarely seen in the UK. But concerns over the regressivity of local taxes have not been restricted to the community charge. Concerns had previously been voiced over the regressivity of the pre-1990 (1989 in Scotland) local tax on households, domestic rates.

Domestic rates were a property tax that was set proportional to 'rateable value'.[2] During the 1960s, the Wilson Government introduced two reforms to address growing concerns that a regressive property tax was imposing an intolerable burden on poorer households. First, means-tested rate relief was introduced to help poorer householders. Second, domestic rate relief grants effectively transferred more of the burden of paying for local spending on to non-domestic ratepayers. The rebate system was subsequently reformed on several occasions, most recently as part of the 1988 Fowler reforms of social security.

The Conservative governments of the 1980s argued that domestic rates were unfair, because those who voted for and received the benefits of local services were not the same as those who paid for them through higher local taxes. This concern about 'marginal

---

[1]Northern Ireland has continued to operate a system of domestic rates in the years since 1990, leaving it beyond the scope of this report.

[2]Roughly speaking, this was based on the rental value of a property at the valuation date, subject to a number of assumptions.

accountability' — that everybody who could vote for higher local spending should pay something towards its cost — led to the introduction of the community charge as a replacement for the domestic rates.

Alongside the new local tax came community charge benefit. It differed from rate rebates in one crucial respect: the poorest individuals only qualified for a maximum rebate of 80 per cent of their community charge, in contrast to the 100 per cent rebates available under the domestic rates. The benefit recipient was liable for the remainder. Twenty per cent of what central government judged a 'standard' community charge bill was refunded through increased income support payments. This fell short of the actual bills faced by most benefit recipients, since a majority of councils set tax rates above this 'standard' level. Collecting relatively small amounts of tax from individuals whose only income was social security benefits proved extremely expensive. It was from the 'fiscal anarchy'[3] of the poll tax period that the council tax was born.

1.2. The Council Tax

Council tax pays for between a fifth and a quarter of local government spending. But since it is the only revenue source over which councils have control, a £1 per head increase in local spending leads to a £1 per head increase in local tax bills (before benefits are taken into account).[4]

The council tax is a hybrid tax, containing elements of a property tax, a personal tax and, via the benefit system, an income tax. The property element works through a system of banded property valuations; the

---

[3]Besley, Preston and Ridge, 1997.
[4]Councils can also run down reserves to finance additional spending.

personal element works through discounts for homes where there are fewer than two residents; and the income element works through council tax benefit, a means-tested benefit.

1.2.1. The property element

The council tax assigns each property to one of eight bands according to its value on 1 April 1991. Banding kept down the cost of the initial valuation exercise and was intended to avoid the need for frequent revaluations, which have always been politically controversial.

Local authorities initially set a council tax rate applying to properties in band D. Properties in other bands pay a nationally fixed proportion of this band D rate. So, for example, households in band A properties pay two-thirds of the council tax paid by band D households, and those in band H pay twice as much. Table 1.1 shows the range of values for each band, the rate of tax relative to band D and the percentage of properties in each band. Band cut-off points were set at lower levels in Scotland and Wales than in England in recognition of the lower property prices prevalent in these countries.

In a few special cases, households are not liable for any council tax due to the nature of the property or its inhabitants. Households consisting solely of students, for example, are exempted from council tax completely. There is also a discount scheme that reduces the basic council tax bill for some people with disabilities.[5]

---

[5]Houses that contain features that meet the specific needs of disabled people are given a single band discount in their council tax liability, unless they are already in band A, in which case no discount is available.

TABLE 1.1

Council tax bands, tax rates and percentage of properties in each band

Band	Capital value range[a]	Proportion of band D tax	Percentage of properties in band
England			
A	< £40,000	6/9	26%
B	£40,000–£52,000	7/9	20%
C	£52,000–£68,000	8/9	22%
D	£68,000–£88,000	1	15%
E	£88,000–£120,000	11/9	9%
F	£120,000–£160,000	13/9	5%
G	£160,000–£320,000	15/9	4%
H	> £320,000	2	< 1%
Wales			
A	< £30,000	6/9	20%
B	£30,000–£39,000	7/9	26%
C	£39,000–£51,000	8/9	20%
D	£51,000–£66,000	1	15%
E	£66,000–£90,000	11/9	12%
F	£90,000–£120,000	13/9	4%
G	£120,000–£240,000	15/9	3%
H	> £240,000	2	< 1%
Scotland			
A	< £27,000	6/9	27%
B	£27,000–£35,000	7/9	26%
C	£35,000–£45,000	8/9	15%
D	£45,000–£58,000	1	11%
E	£58,000–£80,000	11/9	11%
F	£80,000–£106,000	13/9	5%
G	£106,000–£212,000	15/9	4%
H	> £212,000	2	< 1%

[a]Banding is based on 1991 valuation, so band cut-off points are expressed in 1991 prices.

1.2.2. The personal element

The basic council tax bill is effectively made up of 50 per cent for the property itself and then 25 per cent for each of the first two 'visible' adults living within it.[6] So a single-adult household pays 75 per cent of the bill paid by a two-adult household, but a three-adult household

---

[6]Certain groups, such as live-in carers and students, are 'invisible' to the council tax system: they do not give rise to the personal element of the tax.

does not pay any extra. Empty properties are liable for half the basic, 'two-adult' council tax bill.

1.2.3. The income element: why is there a specific benefit for the council tax?

Typically, those concerned with the distribution of income care about the progressivity or regressivity of the overall tax and benefit system, rather than of individual elements within it. Regressive elements within the tax system, such as some excise duties, can be compensated for through the main progressive elements, such as income tax and the benefit system. But council tax is an exception to this pattern — it is the only tax in the British system that has a specific benefit attached to it. This is because poorer households cannot easily be compensated for local variations in tax through nationally uniform benefits.

The council tax is regressive — it represents a greater share of the incomes of poorer households than it does of those of the rich. This is because it does not vary directly with income, and the relationship between household income and property value is not straightforward. Even if this relationship were proportional, the tax would still be regressive because council tax band relativities ensure that bills fall as a proportion of house price as property value increases. Giles and Ridge (1993) showed that the basic structure of the council tax (before benefits are taken into account) is almost as regressive as that of the poll tax.

The council tax is unique in being the only tax for which rates vary significantly according to where you live. Combining a major, regressive, locally varying tax with nationally set benefit rates would leave the poorest households in high-tax areas with less net income than those living in low-tax areas. This is precisely what happened under the poll tax. Even the poorest had to pay 20 per cent of their actual poll tax liability, but income support was only increased by 20 per cent of a nationally 'standard' bill.[7] Poorer residents in areas where the council set a tax rate above this 'standard' were left with net incomes below the level of the income support 'safety net'. Variation in council tax bills across households means that, in the absence of *specific* relief, the post-tax income of even the poorest households will vary, undermining the idea of a national safety net that can meet basic needs.

Since April 1998, the maximum value of benefit has been restricted to the bill paid by residents of a band E property, even if the residents of larger properties are dependent on benefit income. A theoretical case could be made for not paying higher benefits to those who live in more valuable properties since housing is a major element of wealth. But property is a peculiarly illiquid form of wealth, so the tax liabilities that it gives rise to might be hard to finance for those on low incomes. This is particularly true of older individuals who may live in valuable properties but have modest incomes. Also, those living in areas of the country where house prices are generally high may have little realistic chance of living in a low-banded property, especially if they have large families.

The principal rationale for the existence of council tax benefit is the desire to guarantee a nationally

---

[7]This was 20 per cent of the poll tax bill that each council would set if it set its budget equal to its standard spending assessment (SSA) — the amount that central government thought the council had to spend to provide an unspecified 'standard' level of service. In practice, most councils set poll tax bills considerably in excess of this.

uniform minimum income.[8] This is not the same as a nationally uniform minimum standard of living. Living costs vary across the UK, so a national system of cash benefits confers different purchasing power (in terms of goods and services) in different parts of the country. But as long as these differences are not too great, ensuring a uniform minimum income will go a long way towards ensuring a uniform minimum standard of living. Without council tax benefit, though, there would be variation in the disposable incomes of even the poorest because of the different rates of council tax that apply in different localities.

Such variation would not matter if we were interested in providing a minimum level of consumption (including both private purchases and public services) rather than a minimum level of disposable income, as long as the benefits of extra council spending in high-tax areas offset the effects of high tax rates on poorer people. But while many poorer residents receive considerable benefits from the provision of local public services, there is no guarantee that all of them will gain: extra nursery places offer little benefit to childless individuals on low incomes, for example. So extra public spending is unlikely to be a direct substitute for disposable income in guaranteeing a particular minimum level of consumption.

1.3. Variation of Council Tax across Households

We have argued that the key rationale for council tax benefit is that, in its absence, the tax's variability would

---

[8]Of course, focusing on movements around a safety-net level of income involves giving a great deal of weight to marginal changes in income of those close to the safety net. This report assumes that the preservation of a safety net is an important aim of social policy.

imply local differences in the incomes of the poorest. So we compare the relative variability of council tax bills across households with those of two other liabilities for which the state has provided a special system of support: housing benefit and domestic rates.

Council tax bills vary less across households than domestic rate bills did, mirroring the reduction in the variation of spending levels between local councils over time. Figure 1.1 shows that council tax bills in 1995/96 were far less dispersed than domestic rates bills in 1980/81, with far fewer households facing either especially high or especially low bills. Exactly half of ratepayers faced a bill that was between 70 and 130 per cent of the median bill, compared with the two-thirds (66 per cent) of council tax payers who fell within this range.

Housing benefit, which has a similar structure to council tax benefit, compensates households for the

FIGURE 1.1

Dispersion of council tax bills in 1995/96 and domestic rates in 1980/81

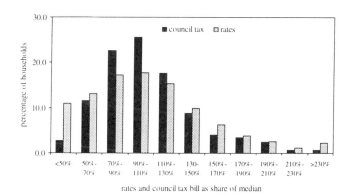

FIGURE 1.2

**Dispersion of rent for housing benefit recipients in 1980/81
and of council tax bills for council tax benefit recipients in 1995/96**

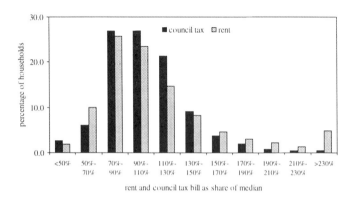

variations in income net of housing costs they would otherwise face due to differences in rents. But housing benefit shields its claimants from a slightly more variable liability since rents are typically far higher than council tax bills (averaging £48 per week compared with under £10 per week) and they are more variable. Figure 1.2 shows that a higher proportion of renters than of council tax payers pay more than double the median bill.

1.4. Council Tax Benefit

Because it is means-tested, council tax benefit works like an income tax for many households. As income rises, benefit entitlement falls. But the benefit's structure is highly complex, with three key elements:

• *Main council tax benefit.* This is calculated by comparing a claimant's council tax liability and the excess of their income over the level that the social security system deems they need. Entitlement to benefit is initially set equal to the bill. It is then reduced on a sliding scale for those with incomes above 'needs'.

- *Non-dependant deductions.* These reduce the householder's council tax benefit entitlement to take account of any incomes earned by other residents of the household.
- *Second-adult rebate.* This typically compensates single householders who are not entitled to main benefit themselves but who share their home with a low-income adult. Without the rebate, such a householder would lose their 25 per cent single-person discount but could not reasonably expect the second adult to contribute to the bill.[9]

The structure of council tax benefit is explained in more detail in Appendix A. Even from the basic features, we can identify problems that potential reforms might seek to rectify:

- *Work incentives.* For every extra £1 of income a benefit recipient has above the level that the social security system deems they need to live, 20p of benefit is lost. This means claimants face an effective marginal tax rate that is 20 percentage points higher than it otherwise would be. This reduces the financial rewards of working.
- *Social security costs of rising rates.* Because maximum benefit is set equal to a family's total council tax, anyone in receipt of benefit will see entitlement rise pound for pound with bills. The

---

[9]In some cases, householders can receive second-adult rebate if it is larger than the main council tax benefit to which they would be entitled — the so-called 'best-buy' comparison.

effect of rising rates on benefit expenditure is made even greater because the higher levels of maximum entitlement they imply mean higher incomes are required to exhaust eligibility, and families previously outside the benefit system are 'floated into' it. The recent trend in council tax rates has been upward, driving increases in expenditure on council tax benefit. Reform might aim to limit the impact that future increases in tax rates will have on benefit spending.

- *Lack of local accountability.* Since benefit recipients are fully compensated for any increase in local council tax bills, they do not face any direct financial incentive to hold their council to account for their stewardship of local revenues.

- *Complexity.* The complexity of the benefit system may reduce take-up as it makes claiming onerous, and it also means that the processing of claims requires provision of a great deal of personal information, which may deter some from applying. This is particularly true of non-dependant deductions and second-adult rebate, which require income assessments of those outside the claimant's immediate family. Furthermore, the complexity of the system is likely to make administrative costs higher and the scope for administrative errors greater than they otherwise would be.

The three elements of the council tax benefit system, each of which involves its own means test, leave us with a means-tested benefit of great complexity. It seems likely that there is a great deal of scope for the system to work rather differently in practice from how its rules imply it should operate in theory.

CHAPTER 2
The Distributional Impact of Council Tax Benefit

This chapter examines who receives council tax benefit for the most recent year for which data are available, 1995/96. First, we examine the effectiveness of the benefit in reducing the burden of council tax for low-income households. Second, we ask why some apparently low-income households do not appear to receive any benefit. Third, we consider the extent to which council tax benefit improves the affordability of council tax for different groups in the population, and which groups are left facing the highest burdens from the tax.

We find that council tax benefit recipients are overwhelmingly in the bottom half of the income distribution and that the benefit succeeds in cutting sharply the average council tax liability of poor families. But we also find evidence that a widespread failure to take up entitlement threatens to undermine the effectiveness of the benefit both in ameliorating the council tax's regressivity and in protecting the income safety net. The problem seems especially acute amongst those on very low incomes.

We find that the unemployed, single parents and social renters are much more likely to receive help from council tax benefit than other people. Single parents are more than eight times more likely to receive benefit than married childless couples. But pensioners and those on low incomes who own their homes outright, who often have little direct contact or experience with other means-tested benefits, receive relatively little help with their council tax bills, largely because they are less likely to take up entitlement.

2.1.   Methods and Data

Official figures can tell us a good deal about who receives council tax benefit. In May 1996, for example, there were 5.614 million recipients of main council tax benefit, of whom 2.717 million were aged over 60 and 2.819 million lived in band A homes. On average, they benefited by £7.28 per week, which covered 86.8 per cent of the average liability of claimants.[10] But the government only keeps the information on recipients that it needs to administer council tax benefit. Consequently, this information has clear limits. It tells us very little about the distribution of the benefit between groups that are not relevant in administrating the system. So it does not allow, for example, comparative analysis of the benefit's effects on different income brackets. Further, these data offer no information on households not receiving council tax benefit, so they reveal nothing about the differences between groups that do and do not claim it.

We can construct a much fuller picture of the operation of council tax benefit than is available from the official figures by using data from the Family Resources Survey (FRS). This has been carried out by the DSS since 1993/94 and uses an in-depth questionnaire, which is answered annually by a nationally representative sample of around 30,000 households. A further benefit of using survey data, such as the FRS, is that it allows us to *model* the operation of the social security system on our sample — so we can compare the council tax benefit that households actually receive with what they should be entitled to. One novel

---

[10]*Social Security Statistics, 1997.*

feature of our work is that we use the actual bill that respondents faced, rather than an average rate for a group of authorities, which is normally used in the FRS to preserve anonymity.

The distribution of claimants by age, council tax band and benefit received amongst the households in the FRS is very similar to that found in official statistics. The FRS suggests that the average payment of council tax benefit to recipients in 1995/96 was £7.93 a week compared to £7.80 in official statistics. It also suggests that there were 5.624 million households on council tax benefit compared to 5.651 million in official statistics.[11] This degree of accuracy gives us confidence in using the FRS to make inferences about household characteristics not included in official figures.

We will assess the effect of council tax benefit on different groups in the population in two main ways. First, we will look at the fraction of various groups who are in receipt of the benefit. Second, we will look at the effect that benefit has on the affordability of the council tax for different groups. To reveal this, we start with households' liability for *gross council tax*, which is simply the bill that they would face if no benefit were received. Next, we calculate the *gross burden* for each group, which is the sum of gross council tax liabilities of all households in a group divided by the sum of their gross incomes. This figure is a measure of how affordable the basic tax is, on average, for households in each group. Finally, we consider *net council tax* — the gross council tax liability of a household minus any benefit it receives — and the *net burden* of each group — total net council tax liability facing a group divided by its total income. The net burden measures the

---

[11]Administrative figures from *Social Security Statistics, 1996*. A detailed comparison of the two sets of data is undertaken in Appendix B.

affordability of the council tax once benefit is taken into account. The gap between the net and gross burdens of a group reveals the extent to which benefit makes the council tax more affordable for its members.

2.2.   Council Tax Benefit and the Income Distribution

In this section, we consider the extent to which council tax benefit succeeds in ameliorating the regressive impact of gross council tax. Households are ranked by 'equivalised' household income, which takes into account that more household income will be needed to provide a given standard of living as the number of household members rises.[12] We group households into 10 equivalised income deciles — so the bottom decile contains the poorest 10 per cent of households, and so on.

FIGURE 2.1

Percentage of households on council tax benefit, by income decile

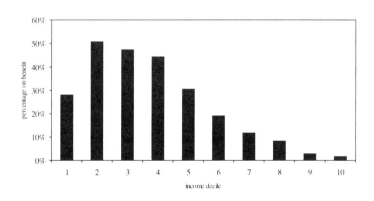

---

[12]This 'equivalisation' is performed using the McClements scale (see McClements (1977)).

FIGURE 2.2

Gross and net council tax burdens, by income decile

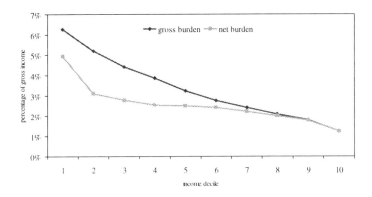

Figure 2.1 shows that, in general, households in poorer deciles are more likely to receive council tax benefit. From the second decile onwards, the fraction of the population on benefit declines as we move up the income distribution. As we would expect, given the means-tested nature of the benefit, the top 20 per cent of the income distribution contains very few households on council tax benefit. But, surprisingly, Figure 2.1 shows that there are relatively few households in the bottom decile receiving council tax benefit — just 20 per cent compared with over 50 per cent in the second decile.

Figure 2.2 shows that the burden of paying gross council tax (as a percentage of income) falls as we move up the income distribution, as is expected since council tax, like most property taxes, is a highly regressive tax. But Figure 2.2 also shows that council tax benefit helps to reduce the extent of this regressivity. Except for the first decile, it reduces the burden by far more for those in the poorest deciles than for those higher up the income distribution. Ignoring the poorest tenth, council

17

tax benefit changes the tax from being very regressive to being a broadly proportional tariff that represents between 2 and 3 per cent of household income for all but the richest.

In spite of means testing, it seems that comparatively little benefit goes to those whom the FRS allocates to the poorest income decile, leaving them facing a burden from the tax that is far higher than that of any other decile. Benefit reduces the average burden of the second decile by around 40 per cent but only cuts the gross burden of the bottom decile by a little over 20 per cent. Since the bottom decile started with a much higher average gross burden than any other decile, it is left with a very large average net burden compared with the other deciles. The net burden is 5 per cent for decile 1, whereas for all other deciles but the richest it lies around 2 or 3 per cent.

2.3.   Does Council Tax Benefit Fail the Poorest Households?

The above evidence from the FRS seems to suggest that council tax benefit is failing a large fraction of the poorest households. We repeated the analysis of Section 2.2 on smaller segments of the income distribution and found that the very lowest levels of receipt of council tax benefit in the bottom half of the income distribution were located at the very bottom of the bottom decile, making the problem seem still more urgent. But interpreting the raw figures in this way could be misleading. First, the 'snapshot' of current income in the FRS may be a poor guide to a household's 'normal' income. Second, many of those entitled to benefit may not have received it at the time of the survey because they were waiting for their claims to be processed. Third, there is, of course, the possibility that council tax benefit itself is simply poorly targeted. We consider each possible explanation in turn.[13]

2.3.1. Are reported incomes sometimes misleading?

The 'snapshot' of income taken at the time the survey was carried out may give a misleading impression of a household's 'normal' income if incomes are variable or paid irregularly or if individuals are moving into or out of work. This is a particular concern for those who are self-employed or have disparate sources of income.

On the basis of the income measure in the FRS, we find a group at the very bottom of the distribution who do not show the characteristics of being permanently poor.[14] Surprisingly, the bottom 2 per cent of the income distribution by net income (after taxes and benefits) turn out to have high average gross incomes. Some of them are making large income tax payments. Some 80 per cent of households in the bottom 2 per cent record non-zero income tax or National Insurance payments, marginally more than in the income distribution as a whole. This is surprising, given the existence of personal allowances within the income tax system and of the lower earnings limit within National Insurance, which should mean a zero tax liability for the very poor. Since liability for income tax is calibrated on an annual basis, this indicates that the FRS measure of income over the last week may be a poor guide to average weekly income over the year as a whole for certain groups. Those with irregular income, such as many of the self-employed, are likely to fit this pattern. Indeed,

---

[13]It is also possible that some householders misrepresent their true income to survey researchers.

[14]We divided households into 50 'bi-centiles' by equivalised household income. It is in the bottom bi-centile (the poorest 2 per cent) that concerns over the accuracy of the FRS income measure as a proxy for 'normal' income are most acute.

we find a concentration of households containing self-employed individuals at the very bottom of the income distribution. But this explanation does not account for the low levels of receipt of the benefit in the higher portions of the bottom decile, all of which have lower proportions on benefit than the second decile, in spite of the fact that these households have very low average tax payments.

One way of checking whether some of those recorded as having very low incomes in the FRS are genuinely poor is to look at their expenditure patterns. Expenditure relates closely to income in the long run, but transient changes in income are unlikely to lead to dramatic changes in expenditure. Households that suffer a fall in income that they know to be temporary might maintain their expenditure, being happy to spend savings or to borrow. Furthermore, the relative well-being of households with large stocks of savings, which might prevent us from wanting to think of them as poor even if they record a low income, might be better judged by their spending (which might be largely financed from savings) than by their income. The Family Expenditure Survey (FES) includes information on both the incomes and the expenditure patterns of an annually representative sample of around 7,000 UK households. Evidence from this suggests a similar relationship between the receipt of council tax benefit and household income to that in the FRS data. In particular, households in the bottom decile are less likely to be in receipt of benefits than those in the second decile.

In Figure 2.3, FES respondent households have been divided into 50 equally sized blocks — called *bi-centiles* — ranked by net income. In the long run, we would expect to observe higher expenditure by those on

FIGURE 2.3

**Gross and net council tax as a share of household expenditure,
by income bi-centile**

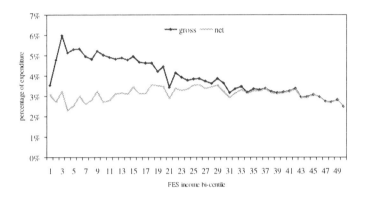

higher incomes. But Figure 2.3 shows that the proportion of expenditure accounted for by gross council tax *increases* over the first three bi-centiles because, on average, household expenditure is *decreasing* over this range. If the apparent low income of many of these households is not affecting their consumption, then the long-run burden for the bottom two income bi-centiles is likely to be much lower than the raw income figures suggest. After the third bi-centile, spending increases with income on average, just as we would expect. So Figure 2.3 shows that the proportion of expenditure accounted for by gross council tax decreases over this range. The net burden of council tax measured as a share of expenditure rather than as a share of income (as it was in Figure 2.2) is broadly proportional across the income distribution.

2.3.2. How many households are waiting to receive council tax benefit?

Many of those on low incomes who do not appear to receive council tax benefit may be in the process of claiming it. Those who have recently become unemployed may accurately report very low or zero current income and non-receipt of council tax benefit. But this may give a misleading impression of the household's welfare because such a state is transitory and will change once the household's claims for council tax benefit and other benefits are resolved.

We find that just over 1 per cent of households (240,000) are in the process of claiming. Such households are especially likely to be on the very lowest incomes: some 60,000 households (6 per cent) in the bottom three income bi-centiles are awaiting the outcome of a claim. But these numbers are too small to provide anything but a partial explanation for non-receipt of benefit in the bottom decile — especially since the top half of the poorest decile shows no particular propensity to be in the process of claiming.

Even accounting for those whose incomes are poorly recorded in the FRS or who are in the process of claiming benefit, there remains a far lower level of benefit receipt in the bottom decile than we would expect. This suggests that some low-income households are failing to receive the help to which they are entitled.

2.3.3. Is council tax benefit entitlement poorly targeted?

It is, of course, possible that the design of council tax benefit means that it fails to target vulnerable groups. To explore this possibility, we used the IFS tax and benefit model, TAXBEN, to tell us how the system *should*

FIGURE 2.4

Entitlement to council tax benefit, by modelled income decile

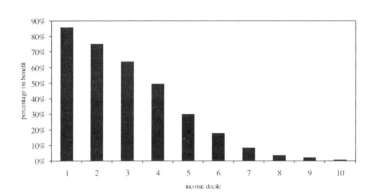

operate, given the rules, abstracting from any take-up problems.[15] Figure 2.4 shows how *entitlement* to council tax benefit varies across the income distribution.[16] In sharp contrast to the pattern of benefit receipt shown in Figures 2.1 and 2.2, entitlement to the benefit is widespread amongst the poorest households.

Figure 2.5 shows what the burden of council tax would look like if everybody claimed their full entitlement to benefit. The modelled gross tax remains regressive, as it was in the FRS data, but the net tax burden looks much more proportional. Indeed, we can see that the net burden actually tends upwards across the first five deciles, which means the tax is progressive over this range.

---

[15]See Giles and McCrae (1995).

[16]For this section, we use 'modelled income' — reported gross income adjusted by modelled tax liability and benefit entitlement. The income deciles have also been reconstructed on the basis of modelled income.

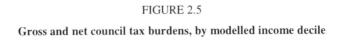

FIGURE 2.5

Gross and net council tax burdens, by modelled income decile

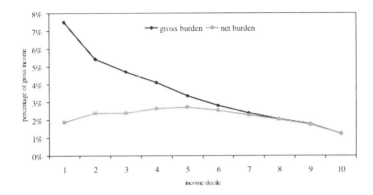

Whilst council tax benefit seems to be designed to target the poorest households fairly effectively, the relationship between income and entitlement is imperfect. Twenty-five per cent of households in the poorest three deciles (around 2 million households) are not entitled to benefit, whilst a similar number of households in the top 60 per cent of the income distribution do get the benefit.

2.4. Households that Do Not Claim Their Council Tax Benefit

A major reason why some of the poorest households do not receive council tax benefit seems to be non-take-up rather than non-entitlement. We estimate the take-up of council tax benefit to be around 70 per cent.[17] We might

---

[17]This differs from DSS estimates of 72–80 per cent (DSS, 1997). DSS figures are produced using a more complex computer algorithm than ours, but its figures are being revised, making direct comparison impossible.

The take-up rate is measured here as the total number of families receiving council tax benefit divided by the sum of numbers receiving and numbers

24

expect take-up to be lower when the amount of benefit that a household could claim is very small, meaning that householders may judge that the hassle of claiming is not worth while. But the DSS estimates that the average weekly unclaimed amount is £5.90 a week, not much less than the average weekly entitlement amongst claimants, which stands at £6.70.[18]

Table 2.1 shows which groups are least likely to take up their benefit entitlement. Non-take-up is most widespread amongst the following:

- *Married pensioners.* Only about half of the married pensioners entitled to the benefit actually receive it. For all other family types, the comparable figure is more than two-thirds.

- *Owner-occupiers.* Less than half those who own their homes outright take up their entitlement to benefit. This leaves over a million households owning their homes outright but not receiving the council tax benefit to which they are entitled. The take-up rate for mortgage-holders is also relatively low, standing at 57 per cent, compared with 84 per cent for social renters.

- *Those who do not receive other benefits.* Receipt of other means-tested benefits is very strongly associated with taking up council tax benefit entitlement. The take-up rate of council tax benefit

---

modelled as entitled but lacking receipt in the FRS. DSS methodology differs slightly from ours in that it takes the number receiving the benefit from administrative statistics whereas we take the number reporting receipt from the FRS, which allows us to produce separate take-up rates for more disaggregated groups. This methodological difference should have little impact on overall results because the total number and the characteristics of council tax benefit recipients found in the FRS are very similar to those found in administrative data.

[18]DSS, 1997.

TABLE 2.1

Take-up of entitlement to council tax benefit
for different classes of household

Category	Take-up rate	Category	Take-up rate
Family type		*Income support?*	
Married pensioners	51%	Someone in receipt	87%
Single pensioners	71%	No one in receipt	52%
Married with children	75%		
Married, no children	68%		
Lone parents	84%		
Single adults	68%		
Tenure type		*Households in receipt of …*	
Social rented	84%	Housing benefit	88%
Private rented	74%	Family credit	65%
Mortgaged	57%	Benefits for severely	81%
Owned outright	48%	disabled people[a]	
Other	48%	Retirement pension	64%
		Unemployment benefit	50%
Total	70%	None of these benefits	38%

[a]Receipt of either component of disabled living allowance, attendance allowance or severely disabled allowance.

is 87 per cent for households where at least one individual is receiving income support; for households not on income support, it is just 52 per cent. The take-up rate amongst recipients of housing benefit, which is claimed using the same form as council tax benefit, is higher still. Receipt of other, non-means-tested, benefits also seems to go alongside better take-up rates: those in receipt of (non-means-tested) benefits for severely disabled people are far more likely to claim entitlement to council tax benefit than the national average. In sharp contrast, for those who have no other contact with the social security system, take-up is very low: it falls to 38 per cent amongst those who do not claim any of the benefits listed in Table 2.1.

Just 4.5 per cent of households with both modelled entitlement to and recorded receipt of council tax benefit are in the bottom income decile, but 41 per cent of those not receiving the entitlement that TAXBEN assigns to them are in this group. This tendency for households with the lowest incomes not to claim explains a good deal of the low levels of receipt that we recorded at the bottom of the income distribution.

It is hard to avoid drawing the conclusion that contact with the broader welfare system has a large impact on take-up of council tax benefit. Those on income support and housing benefit are likely to claim, often simultaneously. Many married pensioners and many people who own their homes outright (who do not qualify for housing benefit) could well have got through their lives having had very little experience with social welfare. The take-up problem of council tax benefit is almost certainly aggravated by its complexity. This reduces the likelihoods that individuals will know that they are entitled to benefit and that they will know how to claim.

The corollary of the take-up problem of a benefit is receipt by the non-entitled. We estimate that just under 3 per cent of the population are receiving council tax benefit without being entitled to it. This amounts to 11 per cent of households that receive the benefit. Receipt without entitlement could reflect a number of things: administrative mistakes, fraud, recent changes in circumstances for households or data problems. The ability of the system to deal with each of these is likely to be reduced when the benefit design is complicated.

2.5.   Who Gets Council Tax Benefit?

Looking at the burden of council tax across the income distribution, we have seen that council tax benefit ensures affordability for many poor households but also that it leaves high net liabilities for many others with low income. But who are these households? In this section, we look at the burden of council tax and the likelihood of receiving council tax benefit across the population grouped by family type, economic status, housing tenure, property value and region. Again, our data come from the 1995/96 FRS throughout this section.

2.5.1. Family type

Table 2.2 shows that over 65 per cent of lone parents receive council tax benefit but that only 8 per cent of married couples without children do. Large fractions of both married and single pensioners also receive the benefit. Generally, couples are much less likely to be on council tax benefit than their single counterparts. Single pensioners are the numerically most important group of benefit recipients.

Figure 2.6 shows the impact of council tax benefit on the affordability of the council tax for each group. The total height of each bar represents the average gross council tax burden for each family type, and the shaded fraction represents benefit received, leaving the dark bar

TABLE 2.2

Numbers of households and percentages on council tax benefit, by family type

Family type	Number of households on benefit (thous.)	Percentage of households on benefit
Married pensioners	565	22%
Single pensioners	1,809	48%
Married with children	613	12%
Married, no children	481	8%
Lone parents	1,003	66%
Single adults	1,180	28%
Total	*5,651*	24%

FIGURE 2.6

Gross and net council tax burdens, by family type

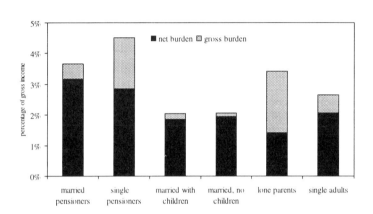

representing the part of the bill that is actually paid — the net burden for each group. The groups with the highest average gross burdens — lone parents and pensioners — have them reduced most by council tax benefit. In contrast, the low gross burden of working-age couples is barely modified by benefit at all.

Although many pensioners receive council tax benefit, they face much higher net burdens than other groups. This is especially true for married pensioners. More than one in five of this group receive some benefit, but the average net burden that the council tax imposes on married pensioners is not much lower than the group's gross burden. This is because a lot of pensioners who claim council tax benefit receive only a partial rebate. Fifty-three per cent of the pensioners receiving benefit still have to pay some council tax, because their incomes are sufficient to bring about some withdrawal of entitlement. Amongst non-pensioners, two-thirds (67 per cent) of households on benefit have their whole bill covered.

2.5.2   Economic status

With the partial exception of part-timers, only a very small fraction of working households receive council tax benefit, as shown in Table 2.3. But a clear majority of those who are unemployed or not working for other reasons receive council tax benefit. In spite of 70 per cent of the unemployed receiving benefit, the unemployed make up a relatively small fraction of the total number of recipients, because far fewer people are classed as unemployed than as pensioners, 'others not working', or sick or disabled.

Figure 2.7 shows that the gross burden of council tax is highest for the three non-working categories, being close to or above 4 per cent for all three. For all working families, other than those that have only part-time workers, the burden is much closer to 2 per cent.

TABLE 2.3

Numbers of households and percentages on council tax benefit, by economic status

Economic status[a]	Number of households on benefit (thous.)	Percentage of households on benefit
Full-time self-employed	65	3%
Full-time employees only	192	4%
1 full-time, 1 part-time	20	1%
1 full-time, 1 not working	90	4%
Part-time workers only	385	27%
Over-60s	2,572	39%
Unemployed	804	70%
Others not working	1,522	66%
Total	*5,651*	*24%*

[a]Households are assigned to these groups according to the status of the family unit (single adult or couple) that heads them. This process is sequential down the table. So if a married person in full-time self-employment heads the household, the household is classed in the top group in the table, regardless of the status of their partner.

FIGURE 2.7

Gross and net council tax burdens, by economic status

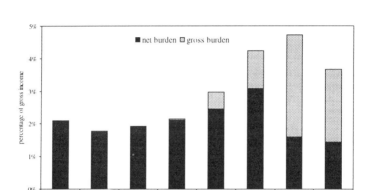

Council tax benefit reduces this disparity. The burden on the unemployed, and others of under 60 who are not working, falls sharply, leaving these groups with the lowest net burden of all. Benefit makes no significant difference to the burden of families containing a full-time worker. As we found before, the benefit system reduces the burden on pensioners but leaves them with the highest net burden.

2.5.3. Housing tenure

Table 2.4 shows that renters, and more particularly social renters, are the most likely housing tenure types to receive council tax benefit. This is hardly surprising since social renters are concentrated 'at the bottom of the income distribution'.[19] Mortgage-holders and people who own their homes outright are more likely to have sufficiently high incomes to exclude them from benefit.

[19]Giles et al., 1996. This report charts the way that various changes in recent decades have left local authority accommodation predominantly occupied by the poorest sections of society.

31

TABLE 2.4

**Numbers of households and percentages on council tax benefit,
by tenure type**

Tenure type	Number of households on benefit (thous.)	Percentage of households on benefit
Social rented	3,397	61%
Private rented	590	34%
Mortgaged	667	7%
Owned outright	940	16%
Other	56	15%
Total	*5,651*	*24%*

The fraction of socially renting households on benefit is so high that, even though less than a quarter of households fall into this group, they constitute a clear majority of recipient households.

Figure 2.8 shows that gross council tax represents a larger share of household income for social renters than for any other tenure group. But council tax benefit reduces this burden by more than for any other tenure group, so social renters are left with the lowest net

FIGURE 2.8

Gross and net council tax burdens, by tenure type

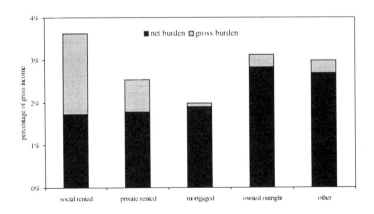

burden of the tax. Mortgage-holders, who tend to be richer, have a low gross burden which is largely unaffected by the existence of council tax benefit. The highest net burdens are faced by those who own their homes outright, who receive little help from council tax benefit. Such people tend to have lower average incomes than mortgage-holders since they are more likely to be pensioners. The average age of householders owning their home outright is 66; the average age of mortgage-holders is 43.

2.5.4. Council tax band

Table 2.5 shows that a far higher proportion of those living in low-banded properties than of those in higher-value properties are on benefit, and each valuation band has a lower proportion on benefit than the next. In band A, nearly half of households receive some benefit, whereas the fraction of band H households on benefit is negligible. Even though council tax liability increases with band, differences in benefit entitlement between bands are chiefly driven by differences in average incomes — there seems little evidence of the higher

TABLE 2.5

Numbers of households and percentages on council tax benefit, by council tax band

Council tax band	Number of households on benefit (thous.)	Percentage of households on benefit
A	2,788	46%
B	1,210	26%
C	878	19%
D	514	14%
E	168	8%
F	70	6%
G	22	3%
H	1	1%
Total	5,651	24%

council tax liability of more expensive homes leading to their owners being 'floated' into benefit entitlement.

In numerical, rather than proportional, terms, the dominance of the low bands amongst claimants is even more marked, because more people live in lower-band homes. Indeed, nearly half of recipient households live in band A homes, far greater than the 23 per cent of households that the FRS suggests live in band A properties overall. The table also suggests that the government's recent introduction of a restriction on the value of council tax benefit to a maximum amount given by the band E bill (which therefore affects only those in council tax bands F and above) will affect fewer than 100,000 households.

Figure 2.9 shows that the average gross burden of the council tax falls successively across bands. The effect of rising incomes across bands easily dominates the effects of the higher bills faced by those in more expensive homes. This is consistent with what we would expect if house values vary proportionately with income because, given the rules of the council tax, bills rise less than proportionally with property values.

The story with the net burden, however, is rather different. The large fraction of households in bands A and B who receive council tax benefit means that the *net* burden for these groups is reduced most sharply. Those in the highest-value homes are scarcely affected by the benefit system, but their incomes are, on average, sufficiently high to leave them with a relatively low net burden. The households that have the highest net burden are those placed in the middle bands — C, D, E and F — with the highest burden of all being found in band E. These bands cover the great bulk of the more expensive half of properties — fewer than 5 per cent of homes are in the top two bands.

FIGURE 2.9

Gross and net council tax burdens, by council tax band

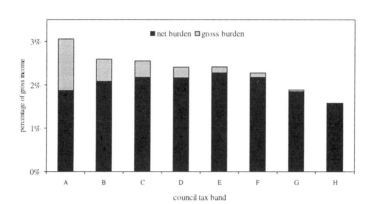

Council tax benefit alters the incidence of the council tax to ensure that the tax *does*, on average, pose a lower burden to most of those in less expensive houses than it does to those in moderately expensive houses.

2.5.5. *Region*

Table 2.6 shows that a larger proportion of people in the country's poorer regions, such as North and North-West, receive benefit than in the more affluent areas, such as the South-East outside London — exactly as we might expect. But there are two exceptions to this pattern. First, in Wales, which has the lowest per capita income in Great Britain, only 27 per cent of households are on council tax benefit. Figure 2.10, which compares average council tax burdens across regions, points to an explanation. In spite of its low average income, Wales has a low gross burden of council tax, which implies that it must have lower average bills than other regions. Lower bills reduce the numbers entitled to council tax benefit by 'floating' people out of benefit entitlement.

TABLE 2.6

Numbers of households and percentages on council tax benefit, by region

Region	Number of households on benefit (thous.)	Percentage of households on benefit
North	432	30%
Yorkshire and Humberside	513	26%
North-West	772	31%
East Midlands	381	23%
West Midlands	543	26%
East Anglia	193	21%
Greater London	802	28%
South-East	740	17%
South-West	402	21%
Wales	337	27%
Scotland	537	27%
Total	*5,651*	*24%*

Second, in London — the UK's highest-income region — a surprisingly high fraction of households receive council tax benefit. In part this is because the income in the capital is very unequally distributed — London contains some pockets of extreme deprivation, such as Hackney and Tower Hamlets, in spite of its high

FIGURE 2.10

Gross and net council tax burdens, by region

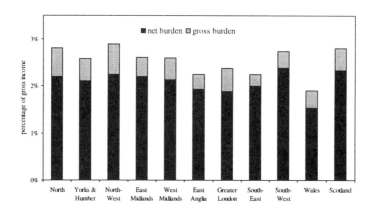

average income. But the high numbers entitled to benefit in London also reflect the effect of its high property prices, which give rise to higher council tax bills and so lead to more people being 'floated' into benefit entitlement.

2.6. Conclusions

Council tax benefit largely succeeds in targeting help towards those who would otherwise face the greatest burdens in paying council tax: social renters, lone parents, pensioners and the workless. But despite the effects of the benefit system, retired people continue to face relatively high net burdens of council tax because of their high average ratios of housing wealth to income and because of the tapering of benefit entitlement.

Although council tax benefit reduces the regressivity of the tax across most of the income distribution, the raw figures suggest a problem at the very bottom of the income distribution. Part of this is due to transitory low incomes and delays waiting for benefit claims to be processed. But it also seems likely that large numbers of households do not claim council tax benefit in spite of entitlement. This is a major concern since this benefit is an important part of the social security safety net. Non-take-up is especially marked amongst people who own their homes outright, married pensioners and households that are not in receipt of income support. Many members of these groups will have had little experience of the complexities of the means-tested benefit system and may either not realise they are entitled to benefit or be put off from applying. The high net burdens of council tax that we found amongst pensioners and outright homeowners are partly the product of their low rates of take-up.

CHAPTER 3
Changes over Time

The burden of council tax will change over time due to variations in council tax rates and socio-economic and demographic trends. This chapter considers how the level and distribution of council tax rates have changed since the introduction of the council tax, and how these changes affected households *abstracting from economic and demographic trends.* We find that council tax rates have risen in real terms every year since 1993[20] and have increased much more quickly in some areas than in others. These increases hit hardest those groups who originally faced the highest burden from the council tax, such as retired people.

3.1. Evolution of Council Tax Rates since 1993

The level and distribution of real council tax rates (after allowing for the effects of inflation) between areas will vary over time for a number of reasons:

- *National trends.* The total value of central government grants to local authorities plays a crucial part in determining the share of local

---

[20]Average band D rates are used as the measure of council tax level.

Sources: For England and Wales — CIPFA (various years).

For Scottish rates in 1993/94 and 1994/95 — CIPFA Scotland (1995 and 1996).

For Scottish rates from 1995/96 onwards — figures from Scottish Office.

Average rates and increases are calculated weighting the bills of authorities by their population. In calculating real increases, the price index used is the retail price index excluding its local tax element.

spending to be paid for by the council tax. The government makes separate decisions on the share of 'standard' spending to be locally financed in England, Scotland and Wales. Slow rates of growth of grants in recent years have put upward pressure on bills, particularly in Scotland and Wales.

- *Grant decisions.* Central government makes decisions about the allocation of grant between individual local councils. Councils that lose grant may choose to maintain spending levels by increasing council tax rates by more than the national average.

- *Local budget decisions.* Over time, councils may vary their spending relative to the centrally determined 'standard level' or standard spending assessment (SSA).[21] For example, in 1997/98, Liverpool spent 13.8 per cent above its SSA, while Westminster spent 13.1 per cent below SSA.

3.1.1. Overall trends

Over the first five years of the council tax, bills increased in cash terms in all but five authorities, while 95 per cent of councils increased their bills in real terms (after allowing for inflation). Over this period, the average band D rate increased from £561 in the first year to £752 in 1998/99. This amounts to a nominal increase of 34 per cent — a 16.5 per cent increase in real terms.[22] Table 3.1 charts how these increases have

---

[21]Standard spending assessment is the level of spending that central government infers that each local authority requires, using regression techniques on councils' characteristics to compare 'needs'. Grant is then distributed to ensure that all councils spending at SSA will set identical tax rates.

[22]The overall increase figures relate the average council tax rate in 1993/94 to that in 1998/99; they differ from the product of the annual increases in

TABLE 3.1

Average annual increases in council tax bills

	Nominal increase on previous year	*Real increase on previous year*[a]
1994/95	3.0%	0.4%
1995/96	5.7%	2.4%
1996/97	7.4%	5.0%
1997/98	7.0%	4.6%
1998/99	8.5%	4.4%

[a]Nominal increase divided by RPI inflation (excluding its council tax element).

taken place since the council tax was introduced. The upward trend in tax rates has been especially sharp in the last three years.

The distribution of council tax rates across the country has become less dispersed over this period. The

FIGURE 3.1

Relationship between bill in April 1993 and subsequent change

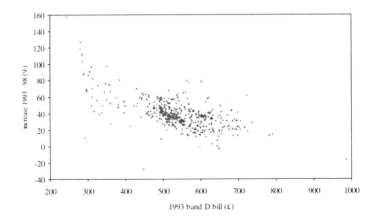

Table 3.1 because the latter figures relate to change between the different individual averages constructed for each year.

scatter plot in Figure 3.1 shows that those councils that set the largest initial council tax rates in 1993/94 had the smallest increase over the next five years, leading to some convergence of tax rates. This may reflect the operation of the capping system, which typically allowed councils that initially spent highly relative to SSA less scope for tax rises, limiting the ability of local budget decisions to affect council tax rates.

3.1.2. England, Scotland and Wales

In the first five years of council tax, bills rose much more quickly in Scotland and Wales than in England, albeit from a lower base. Table 3.2 shows that the biggest increases in Scotland were concentrated in two years — 1996/97 and 1997/98 — whereas Welsh bills have risen more quickly than those in England every year. Over the five years, all Welsh and Scottish taxpayers faced real increases in tax bills, while the residents of 23 English districts saw their council tax rates fall in real terms.

Figure 3.2 shows the effect that differential rates of growth in council tax rates have had on the relative size of the average band D rate in each country.[23] When the council tax was introduced, Scotland, and more

TABLE 3.2

**Mean annual increases in band D rates
in England, Scotland and Wales**

	England	*Scotland*	*Wales*
1994/95	3.2%	4.8%	7.7%
1995/96	5.1%	6.1%	11.8%
1996/97	6.0%	14.6%	18.1%
1997/98	6.8%	10.7%	6.9%
1998/99	9.4%	5.7%	12.3%

[23]It should be borne in mind that the band D rate applies to houses with higher values in England than in Scotland and Wales.

41

FIGURE 3.2

Changing average council tax band D rates
in England, Scotland and Wales

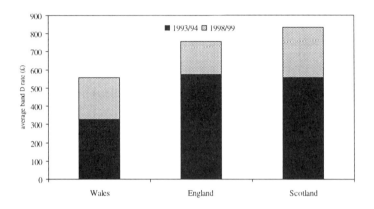

particularly Wales, faced significantly lower council tax rates than England. But by 1998/99, the average Scottish band D rate (population weighted) had risen above the English figure. The average Welsh band D rate now represents a much higher share of the English average than it did in 1993/94, but it is still lower.

3.2. Regional Impact of Council Tax Rises

The overall burden of the council tax, as well as its particular effects on different groups, may change over time due to changes in council tax bills or to changes in households' financial circumstances. We abstract from underlying changes in economic conditions, such as falling unemployment and rising real average incomes, to isolate the effect of changing council tax rates on the underlying affordability of the council tax. Using TAXBEN — the IFS tax and benefit model — we impose each year's council tax rates on households in the 1995/96 FRS, showing the effect this would have had on them *if their own financial circumstances had not changed over the period*. We uprate all council tax bills and the incomes of all households to 1998 to take account of inflation, and we use the 1998/99 tax and benefit system throughout.[24] As well as charting the effect on the burden the council tax imposes, we draw out the implications of increasing bills for the numbers entitled to benefit.

Figure 3.3 shows that the average gross burden of the council tax has increased in every region, with the largest increases being in Scotland and Wales, where council tax rates have increased most quickly. Scotland has moved from having the third-highest gross burden to having the highest burden of all. But despite the steep

FIGURE 3.3

Gross council tax burden, by region

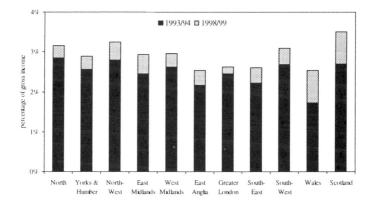

---

[24]The use of a constant benefit system means that we are also abstracting from any changes to the rules of council tax benefit, but the only example of such change is the band E restriction, which has had minimal distributional impact.

rises in Welsh tax bills, average gross burdens in Wales remain the lowest in Britain because tax rates were initially so low. In 1993/94, the average Welsh burden was significantly less than 2 per cent of income, by far the lowest in Britain. But by 1998/99, the average burden had risen to 2.5 per cent, the same as in East Anglia and comparable to that in several other English regions.

Figure 3.4 shows the average net burdens of council tax in each region in 1993/94 and 1998/99. Even after five years, the Welsh continued to face the lowest net burden: low average incomes in Wales ensure that it attracts more help from the benefit system than relatively prosperous English regions that also have low gross council tax burdens. Within England, increases in the net council tax burden have been fairly uniform across regions. But the relatively low increase in London has seen its gross burden fall relative to other regions — it now has the fourth lowest.

FIGURE 3.4

Net council tax burden, by region

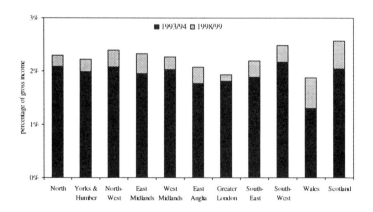

Increases in council tax rates since 1993/94 have been the driving force behind rising council tax benefit expenditure. We estimate that they added 20 per cent in real terms to the cost of the benefit, when considered in isolation. Spending on council tax benefit increases more than proportionately with council tax bills, since higher bills not only produce exactly offsetting increases in benefit for existing recipients but also 'float' extra households on to benefit. TAXBEN calculates that the period's tax rate changes increased the number of households entitled to benefit by 4 per cent. Figure 3.5 shows that every region has seen increases in the proportion of households entitled to benefit since 1993/94, with the increases particularly pronounced in Scotland and Wales, corresponding to their larger increases in council tax rates.

FIGURE 3.5

Percentage of households on benefit, by region

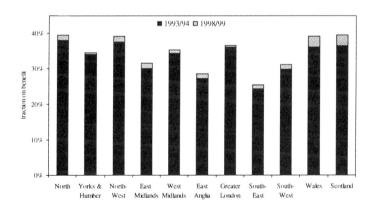

45

3.3. Distributional Impact of Rising Council Tax Bills

Year-on-year increases in council tax rates have increased the net burden of council tax across the whole income distribution. But Figure 3.6 shows that the *modelled* burden (which assumes 100 per cent take-up) has increased most for those in the middle deciles of the income distribution, where the net modelled burden was already highest. The evidence of low take-up that we found in Chapter 2 implies that the effect of the increasing net burden will be much more keenly felt at the bottom of the income distribution than Figure 3.6 would suggest.

As Figure 3.7 shows, the biggest increases in benefit entitlement over the first five years of the council tax occurred in deciles 2 to 4. Entitlement hardly rose in the bottom decile since most people there have incomes at or below income support levels and so have always

FIGURE 3.6

Net council tax burden across the income distribution

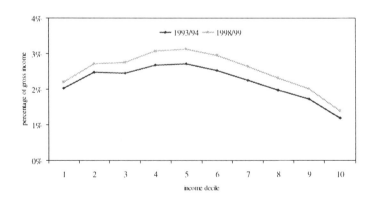

FIGURE 3.7

Distribution of benefit entitlement across the income distribution

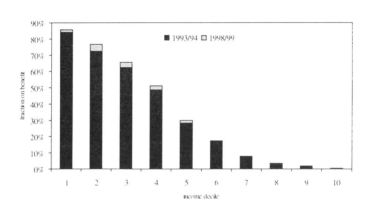

been entitled to a 100 per cent rebate regardless of the size of the bill. In contrast, many households in deciles 2 to 4 are on incomes that put them in or close to that range of income where council tax benefit is being tapered away. For people whose incomes are just too high to qualify for benefit under 1993/94 council tax rates, modest increases in bills will 'float' them into benefit entitlement.

Over time, the net burden of council tax increased less for those groups whose members were most likely to be entitled to full benefit. Table 3.3 shows that, between 1993/94 and 1998/99, the net burden of council tax rose by only 0.2 percentage points for social renters, by 0.1 percentage points for lone parents and by even less for the unemployed. But it rose by 0.4 percentage points for couples without children.

The increase in the fraction of people on benefit is especially marked both for retired people and for households headed by part-time workers. These groups

TABLE 3.3

Effects of the change in council tax rates, 1993/94 to 1998/99

Percentage of income

	Modelled burden of gross council tax benefit		Modelled burden of net council tax benefit		Percentage entitled to benefit	
	1993/94	*1998/99*	*1993/94*	*1998/99*	*1993/94*	*1998/99*
Family type						
Couple pensioner	3.8%	4.4%	2.7%	3.1%	40.7%	42.2%
Single pensioner	4.5%	5.2%	2.5%	2.8%	62.0%	64.3%
Couple with children	2.0%	2.4%	1.8%	2.1%	14.3%	15.7%
Couple without children	2.0%	2.4%	1.8%	2.2%	11.5%	12.7%
Lone parent	3.4%	4.0%	1.2%	1.3%	73.2%	74.3%
Single adult	2.5%	2.9%	1.9%	2.1%	36.9%	37.8%
Economic status						
Self-employed	2.1%	2.5%	1.9%	2.2%	14.3%	16.8%
Full-time employees	1.7%	2.0%	1.7%	2.0%	4.6%	4.8%
1 full-time, 1 part-time	1.9%	2.2%	1.9%	2.2%	0.6%	0.8%
1 full-time, 1 unwaged	2.1%	2.5%	2.1%	2.5%	2.8%	4.4%
Part-time	3.1%	3.6%	2.5%	2.8%	35.0%	38.2%
Retired	4.2%	4.9%	2.6%	2.9%	55.3%	57.3%
Unemployed	4.7%	5.4%	0.8%	0.8%	85.8%	86.4%
Other unwaged	3.9%	4.5%	1.2%	1.4%	77.7%	79.0%
Tenure type						
Social rented	3.8%	4.4%	1.6%	1.8%	68.1%	69.9%
Private rented	2.5%	2.8%	1.6%	1.8%	42.1%	43.3%
Mortgaged	1.9%	2.3%	1.8%	2.1%	11.5%	12.3%
Owned outright	3.1%	3.6%	2.5%	2.9%	30.3%	32.2%
Other	2.9%	3.4%	2.4%	2.7%	27.1%	28.9%

are more likely to have incomes that leave them either on the taper or just above it. Any increase in bill, and corresponding increase in benefit entitlement, is thus especially likely to 'float' on significant fractions of these groups — those people whose income had left them just failing to qualify for any help with council tax in 1993/94.

3.4.   Conclusions

Sharp rises in council tax bills, especially in Scotland and Wales, have brought about significant increases in the net burden of council tax facing households and in the numbers entitled to claim benefit. Those who initially faced the highest net burden of council tax — pensioners, people owning their homes outright and those living in moderately expensive properties — have seen the share of their income taken up by the tax rise especially fast. Under the assumption of 100 per cent take-up, we find that the increase in council tax burden is greatest in the middle of the income distribution. Indeed, rising bills will be very keenly felt amongst households that do not have high incomes but that are typically not sufficiently poor to be entitled to any assistance in meeting their council tax liabilities. In practice, though, low levels of receipt of council tax benefit at the bottom of the income distribution are likely to mean that increases in council tax will hit hard some of those on very low incomes as well.

Although our results abstract from real income growth, the average real-terms increase in tax rate of 16.5 per cent is large enough to have outstripped real rises in household incomes in the last five years, which means that, on average, the share of council tax in households' total incomes has increased. Last year's Comprehensive Spending Review projected further real increases in local tax revenues over the next few years. But our analysis suggests that the ability to increase council tax revenues indefinitely may be limited by the burden that such increases would impose on those groups already facing the highest net burden of council tax.

CHAPTER 4
Reforms to Council Tax Benefit

We have shown that, while council tax does a good deal of what it is intended to do, there are a number of concerns with the present system: its rising cost, its effect on work incentives, its breaking of the link between benefit recipients' bills and their net income, and its great complexity and take-up problems.

In this chapter, we use TAXBEN to assess whether a range of possible reforms could alleviate one or more of these problems without compromising the strengths of the current system. The reforms considered are: first, abolishing council tax benefit and compensating low-income households through other, existing, means-tested benefits (reform 1); second, replacing council tax benefit with exemptions for vulnerable groups or capping how much of a household's income can be taken up by council tax, as occurs in some other countries (reforms 2 and 3); third, making changes to the current structure of council tax by abolishing second-adult rebates or non-dependant deductions, by restricting benefit entitlement to that of a band B property or by ceasing to compensate householders for local variations in tax rates (reforms 4 to 7); fourth, reforming the council tax itself by cutting its overall take or increasing the progressivity of the band structure (reforms 8 and 9). For each reform, we present a brief outline of the objectives of the reform and the changes that would be required in the social security system.[25]

---

[25]A full series of results from the various modelled reforms is available from the authors.

We assess the impact of each reform against a number of criteria:

- *Cost.* Whilst council tax benefit makes up a relatively small share of the social security budget, its cost is growing. Any gains from reforms that increase total spending need to be compared with the benefits from spending the money in different ways. The impact of any reform on the costs of administrating the system also need to be considered. Experience with the community charge suggests that collecting small amounts of money from low-income households is not always cost-effective.
- *Simplicity.* We might expect that the complexity of the current system increases the scope for administrative delay and error, as well as fraud. Most worryingly, it may discourage take-up.
- *Distributional issues.* One consideration is the preservation of a nationally uniform disposable income safety net which the current system seeks to defend. In assessing the results of reforms, the key test of the extent to which the safety net is compromised is the number and nature of households losing from the change. We model distributional effects on the assumption of 100 per cent take-up of benefit entitlement, so the analysis of the impact of reforms needs to be coloured by whether those losing would actually claim the benefit under the present system. But even if certain groups would not lose out in practice because they do not claim their current entitlement, many of these non-claimants are genuinely needy. Abolishing entitlement would be a rather unattractive way of dealing with the real distributional problem of non-take-up.

- *Accountability.* The 1986 Green Paper on local government finance argued that there was a problem when there was a difference between those who use, those who vote for and those who pay for local services (DoE, 1986). The present government also argues that a clear link between the spending decision made by a local council and the council tax bill that comes through the door is an important element of local accountability (DETR, 1998).
- *Work incentives.* The withdrawal of means-tested benefits as incomes rise can cause disincentives for individuals to move into paid work or to work longer hours. Evidence cited in the publications accompanying the 1997 Pre-Budget Report suggested that the expected loss of council tax benefit plays a particularly crucial role in deterring people from entering the labour market.[26] Thirty-two per cent of income support recipients surveyed gave loss of council tax benefit as a factor putting them off returning to work, making it a more significant deterrent against taking a job than any other factor except for concern about low wages.

4.1. Reform 1: Increase Income Support Rates

Abolish council tax benefit and spend an equivalent amount on increasing the personal components of income support and means-tested job-seekers' allowance.

This reform is the most radical — abolishing council tax benefit completely and compensating those on low incomes by increasing existing income-related benefits, principally income support. This is the main UK safety-net benefit, aimed primarily at those out of work. At a

---

[26]Shaw et al., 1996.

stroke, this reform would massively simplify the benefit system by reducing the number of different means-tested benefits available to families.

Abolishing local tax relief might also be advanced as making for a clearer link between council tax bills and net income — a link the current council tax benefit removes for its recipients. But any value put on the strengthening of this relationship would have to be carefully weighed against the reality of having to collect monies from low-income households, a process that proved arduous and inefficient under the community charge.

Revenue-neutrality would allow weekly income support rates to be increased by £11.90 for couples and £8.90 for single people. Benefit rates for single individuals are raised by only 75 per cent of the increase for couples, in recognition of their 25 per cent discount in council tax bills. No changes are made to any other parts of the social security system under this reform.

Results

Not surprisingly, this radical reform would affect large numbers of households. Fourteen per cent of households (3.3 million) lose more than £1 per week, and the same number of families gain by more than £1 per week. Figure 4.1 shows that the majority of households in the population are unaffected by this reform but there is significant redistribution of income in the bottom three deciles. Further, there are many more losers than gainers in the bottom decile, and, on average, the lowest two deciles lose £1.36 and £0.45 respectively per week, whereas there are small average gains for all other deciles.

FIGURE 4.1

**Percentages of gainers and losers, by income decile,
from replacing council tax benefit with increased income support rates**

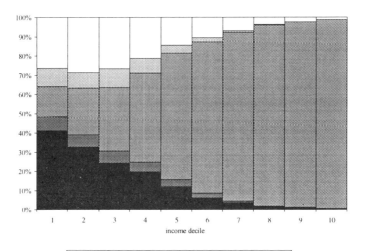

Replacing council tax benefit with a flat-rate increase in income support would lead to considerable redistribution between groups in the population. The most important effects would include:

- Residents of high-council-tax areas would lose out: the benefit system would no longer compensate them for their higher bills. Low-income residents of lower-tax areas would correspondingly gain.

- Current recipients of partial council tax benefit (i.e. those with incomes a little above the level that the social security system deems they need) would tend to lose out. A majority of pensioners who receive council tax benefit only receive partial benefit and would therefore lose from this reform. Part-time workers are another group with widespread receipt of partial rebates, so they would also lose out.

- Recipients of income support who are not liable for the council tax, such as jobless grown-up children who live with their parents, would gain through the income support increase.

Effects on the financial incentives to work would be mixed:

- The financial incentive *to move into work* would be blunted because the loss of council tax benefit would go uncompensated for those working more than 16 hours a week, because they are not eligible for income support. For low-wage workers, in-work income would therefore fall relative to the benefit income available out of work.
- Those already in work would keep more of any increase in income since (as they would receive no benefit) higher incomes would no longer result in loss of benefit. This might lead employees to choose to work more hours.

The large number of low-income losers from this reform — many of them pensioners and working families with children — makes it politically unattractive. But many of its worst effects could be tackled by minor modifications to other means-tested benefits without forgoing too much simplicity.

Modifications

There are three effects of the basic reform that minor modifications to other means-tested benefits could be used to attempt to alter — the large total number of low-income losers, the losses amongst working families with children and the large numbers of pensioners sustaining losses.

First, the huge number of very-low-income losers that the basic reform produces is largely the product of the inefficiency of using straight increases in income support to compensate for the loss of council tax benefit. This inefficiency reflects the large amount of revenue being diverted to income support recipients who face no council tax liability and so require no compensation for the loss of benefit. Introducing a 'head-of-household premium' to income support would enable the funds released by abolishing council tax benefit to be targeted at those who would normally be liable for paying the bill. On a revenue-neutral basis, this would mean more households in the bottom income decile gained than lost out from the abolition of council tax benefit. But, none the less, average losses in the bottom decile of 93p per week persist, and it remains the case that over a quarter (27.6 per cent) of households in the bottom three deciles face losses of over £1 a week.

The actual (as opposed to modelled) distributional implications of this reform may not be very different from what actually happens at present, since 50 per cent of the modelled 'losers' do not currently claim their benefit entitlement. But many of these non-claimants are genuinely needy, and abolishing entitlement would be a rather unattractive way of dealing with the real distributional problem of non-take-up.

Second, the dampening effect of the basic reform on the financial incentive to work of those with children might be a particular concern. Out-of-work benefit incomes are typically higher relative to incomes in work for this group than for the childless. They therefore already face less financial incentive to enter work than other groups, and abolishing the council tax benefit available in work may aggravate this situation. Combining scrapping council tax benefit (where the main compensation is through the income support 'householder premium') with an increase in the generosity of the working families' tax credit would help by targeting extra money at low-income working families with children. Adding a £7 per week increase in the basic working families' tax credit (accompanied by an increase in the taper from 55 per cent to 60 per cent[27]) to the package would leave significantly more working lone parents and one-earner couples gaining. Consequently, it would help to maintain the financial incentives to enter, or to remain in, work for both lone parents and couples. But 7 per cent of lone parents and 12 per cent of single-earner families would still lose out significantly. The exchequer cost of the package would rise to around £180 million (equivalent to a 5.5 per cent rise in council tax benefit expenditure).

The final group losing from the basic reform that we might attempt to give special attention to through the means-tested benefit system is pensioners, but helping this group without major restructuring of other benefits proves more difficult. Neither small increases in income support rates nor relaxation of its capital rules[28] significantly reduce the core of pensioners losing out from the abolition of council tax benefit. This is because of the concentration of pensioners on income levels that are low enough to produce some entitlement to council tax benefit but significantly above income support levels. A radical restructuring of income support,

---

[27]The increase in the taper would ensure that the new generosity did not lead to new (higher-income) families being 'floated' onto benefit.

[28]The capital rules are relaxed so that income support can be received by those with capital of up to £16,000 — the current threshold for council tax benefit — instead of up to £8,000.

involving a move away from a 100 per cent withdrawal rate, is what would really be needed to help this group.

Increasing the overall level of benefit spending

Even if all the modifications to other means-tested benefits we have looked at were undertaken alongside the abolition of council tax benefit, over a quarter of households in the bottom three income deciles would continue to lose significantly. Without a big overall increase in benefit spending, it will simply not be possible to compensate all those who lose out from the abolition of council tax benefit. Doubling the cost of council tax benefit entitlement (modelled at £3.2 billion) would allow the 'head-of-household premium' on

FIGURE 4.2

Percentages of gainers and losers, by income decile, from scrapping council tax benefit but spending double its cost on income support for heads of households

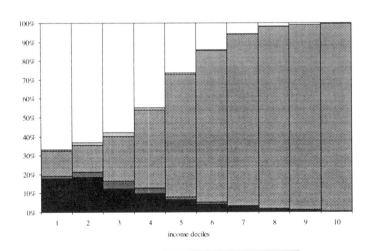

income support to be set to £25 for couples and £18.75 for singles, as well as covering the increase in the working families' tax credit and the relaxation of income support's capital rules that we have already modelled. This package would redistribute large amounts of money to the bottom third of the income distribution. The average gain in the bottom decile would be £6.66 per week, an increase of nearly 6 per cent in its average net income. But even with this dramatic increase in spending, 10 per cent of households still lose out from the abolition of council tax benefit, including 20 per cent of the bottom two income deciles, as shown in Figure 4.2.

It is thus very difficult to see how council tax benefit can be abolished without leading to either large numbers of losers amongst vulnerable groups or a significant increase in benefit expenditure, or, indeed, both. We therefore model a number of reforms that recognise that regressive local taxes need *specific* remedies.

4.2.   Reform 2: Exempt Vulnerable Groups

Abolish council tax benefit and exempt pensioners, poorer lone parents, sick and disabled people and some unemployed people from council tax (as is currently the case for students).[29]

Surveying the local tax systems of the European Union, we find that no other member state operates such a complex and comprehensive system of income-related local tax rebates as the UK.[30] Some US states and EU member states such as France operate much simpler

---

[29]We model entitlement to exemption via qualification for certain benefits such as sickness and disability benefits, contributions-based job-seekers' allowance and lone-parent-rate income support. The list of exemptions is similar to that used in some US states. See Raimondo (1992).

[30]Committee of the Regions, 1996.

schemes by simply providing blanket discounts and exemptions to 'vulnerable groups'.

Exemptions for vulnerable groups would be much simpler to administer than the current system, reducing running costs and the scope for administrative error and fraudulent claims. Apart from lone parents, all the groups would qualify for the exemption automatically without having to go through any means test, so that we have moved as radically as possible away from the current income-related council tax benefit. Simplicity would also spread knowledge of entitlement, while the reduced need for means testing would be expected to reduce stigma. Both these effects should encourage increased take-up. Universal benefits, such as child benefit, have much higher take-up rates than means-tested benefits.

Results

The most striking result of the exemption scheme is cost — over £6 billion, roughly twice the cost of council tax benefit. Many households that previously did not qualify for council tax benefit, since they were not poor, would be exempt from the tax, bringing down the average net burden of most groups. But alongside these gainers are a large number of poor families that stand to lose out because they do not fall into any of the 'vulnerable groups'.

The main gainers and losers are as follows:

- Pensioners gain since they are all now exempt from paying council tax.
- Single-earner couples and unwaged couples without children also gain on average — perhaps because these groups contain a relatively high proportion of

sick and disabled people, who would now be exempt from council tax.

• Working lone parents and single childless earners lose out, reflecting the largely uncompensated loss of benefit for employees with low earnings.

• Unemployed people on means-tested job-seekers' allowance lose as they no longer qualify for an automatic 100 per cent rebate. But those on contribution-based benefit gain because they now receive an exemption regardless of their income and/or capital stock, which would previously have prevented some of them from being entitled.

Figure 4.3 shows that exemptions for vulnerable groups leave the net council tax *more* regressive at the bottom of the income distribution and that the net burden of the tax falls in every income decile except the poorest. Despite the large net exchequer cost, those in the poorest decile see little gain on average because of

FIGURE 4.3

Change in net burden across the income distribution following replacement of council tax benefit with exemptions

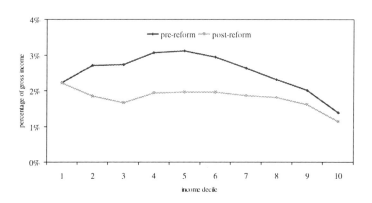

their high average level of entitlement to benefit under the existing system. But while 27 per cent of households in the bottom decile gain more than a pound a week, 19 per cent lose more than a pound a week. This large fraction of losers amongst the poorest households is a concern. The burden of the net council tax is reduced most in the middle part of the income distribution, where many households are in exempt categories but few are currently entitled to help with their council tax bill.

The effects on work incentives are mixed. Those already in work face a sharpened incentive to increase their hours, as, under the reformed system, benefit is no longer withdrawn as earnings rise. For some groups, such as people with disabilities, the incentive to move into work is also sharpened, as they are guaranteed a complete exemption regardless of their income or employment. But for others, moving into work becomes less attractive: the exemption of lone parents and those on contributory job-seekers' allowance is conditional on *not* working more than 16 hours a week.

4.3.   Reform 3: Replace Council Tax Benefit with a 'Circuit Breaker'

Abolish council tax benefit and cap council tax liability at 3.25 per cent of gross household income.

While exemptions for vulnerable groups would largely remove means testing from the council tax system, some US states extend means testing further up the income distribution. Laws in some US states set a maximum percentage of gross household income that households can pay in local property taxes — the so-called 'circuit breaker'. This means that property taxes effectively become income taxes for all households that qualify for the circuit breaker. This conceptually simple reform would be very expensive to administer, but it could be expected to tackle the council tax's regressivity over the top two-thirds of the income distribution, which council tax benefit is not designed to do. We model a revenue-neutral reform that combines the abolition of council tax benefit with a circuit breaker that limits council tax payments to 3.25 per cent of gross household income.

Results

A circuit breaker would redistribute from the poorest households to those in the middle of the income distribution. Figure 4.4 shows that the affordability of the tax would be increased in the middle of the income distribution, where net council tax burdens are currently highest, since many households that previously did not qualify for benefit would see their council tax bills

FIGURE 4.4

Change in net burden across the income distribution under the circuit breaker

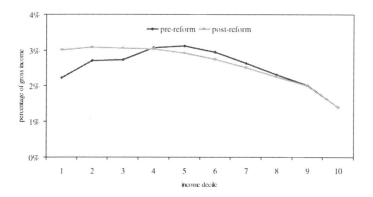

capped at 3.25 per cent of income. But the net council tax liability of the poorest third of households would rise, since all would be expected to make some contribution to local taxes whereas many were previously entitled to a 100 per cent rebate. The top two deciles are largely unaffected as their incomes tend to be too large for them to qualify for either council tax benefit or help from the circuit breaker.

Important gainers and losers include the following:

- Households headed by an employee gain on average, since many benefit from the circuit breaker but very few would be entitled to council tax benefit.
- The unemployed and lone parents lose out on average, since large numbers of both groups are currently entitled to 100 per cent rebate but under the circuit breaker they would have to pay some council tax.
- Pensioner couples end up better off on average, while single pensioners, who are more likely to be on council tax benefit, are left marginally worse off.
- Outright homeowners and residents of higher-valued properties make average gains, as the reform limits the burden arising from their more valuable homes. At the same time, renters and those assigned to low council tax bands lose on average.

A relatively high proportion (74 per cent) of those modelled as losing more than £1 a week from this reform are recorded as claiming council tax benefit in the FRS. Changes to notional entitlement thus relate more closely to the likely real effects of a circuit breaker than to the likely real effects of some other reforms. Losses may be judged especially serious as a result.

Circuit breakers may sound simpler than the complex rules that govern council tax liability, but they are unlikely to be much easier to operate. Councils would have to collect income data on a much larger group of households than they need to in implementing council tax benefit. Small amounts of tax would need to be collected from those on low incomes — the cause of considerable administrative costs and compliance problems during the community charge era.

Circuit breakers would reduce the highest overall marginal withdrawal rates of the current benefit system, since council tax benefit would no longer be withdrawn at 20 per cent as income rose. Instead, liability for the council tax would rise by just 3.25p for every pound of income gained, until income is at such a level that the full value of the council tax is less than 3.25 per cent of income. For those not currently on council tax benefit who would be entitled to help through the circuit breaker, this would amount to an increase of 3.25 percentage points in marginal tax rate.

All households whose tax payments are limited by the circuit breaker effectively pay a flat rate of tax. This would leave the relationship between council tax rates and tax actually paid weaker than before, as many more families would be covered by the circuit breaker than by council tax benefit.

Given the dangers associated with radical reform, we now consider the effects of a more incremental series of reforms that attempt to simplify the current council tax benefit system. We consider the impact of abolishing second-adult rebates and non-dependant deductions and of restricting variation in benefit payments, perhaps through limiting benefit entitlement to what it would be if each council spent at a 'standard' level prescribed by central government, or by capping payments at the level awarded to those in less valuable homes.

4.4. Reform 4: Abolish Second-Adult Rebate

> Abolish the second-adult rebate, so householders no longer receive help on behalf of poorer individuals who share their property.

Council tax benefit is complicated, and second-adult rebate (SAR) is one of the least understood bits of the system. SAR extends the logic of the council tax's personal element to the benefit system by trying to ensure that a single person who shares their home with a low-income second adult does not pay more council tax than they would if they lived alone. The underlying assumption is that the second adult would normally compensate the householder for the loss of his or her single-adult discount, but that their low income leaves them unable to. So the benefit system compensates the householder directly. As a result, individuals who are not themselves poor can claim SAR. Even the richest of single householders could claim for an unemployed adult son or daughter, even if the household, overall, is far from poor.

Abolishing SAR would remove a layer of complexity from council tax benefit and would have a limited distributional effect in practice because take-up is so low — 20 per cent by caseload and 40 per cent by expenditure.[31] Bryson and Smith (1996) found widespread dissatisfaction with the complexity of the claims process and imperfect comprehension of the benefit amongst existing recipients. Low take-up is likely to reflect this complexity. Since many potential claimants are non-poor, they are unlikely to have any

---

[31]DSS, 1997.

direct contact with the rest of the means-tested benefit system.

Results

Abolishing SAR would be a relatively modest reform with relatively modest effects. Savings would be small due to limited entitlement and even more limited take-up. Of the 300,000 who would lose entitlement of more than £1 a week, just 22 per cent currently claim the benefit. The DSS puts the rebate's cost in 1995/96 at just £8.9 million, less than 0.5 per cent of total council tax benefit expenditure, but abolition would save even less, as the poorest existing recipients would, automatically, be partially compensated for losing SAR through main council tax benefit.

The distributional consequences of abolishing the benefit would not be very dramatic — just 1 per cent of households lose out and these are concentrated in the middle of the income distribution since most poorer households are entitled to main council tax benefit and the highest-income households are unlikely to contain low-income individuals. Lone parents and single adults would be the losers from the reform, since couples are not entitled to SAR.

Abolishing the rebate would reduce the complexity of the system. But it could also discourage single householders from allowing poorer adults to share their home, since they would no longer be compensated for their loss of the single-person discount.

4.5.   Reform 5: Abolish Non-Dependant Deductions

No longer reduce main council tax benefit to take account of the income of non-dependants.

A second highly complex aspect of council tax benefit is non-dependant deductions (NDDs). Like the second-adult rebate, NDDs are based on the premiss that additional household members contribute towards paying council tax. They reduce the benefit entitlement of householders who claim main council tax benefit in the light of the contribution that non-dependants could be expected to make to the household bill. Abolishing non-dependant deductions would reduce the complexity of the council tax benefit system and eliminate the problems caused by requiring applicants to provide information on the finances of co-residents outside their immediate family. It would also reverse the trend of government policy over recent years, which has been to increase sharply the rates of NDDs.

Results

Again, this reform would have relatively modest effects. Abolishing NDDs would cost £150 million. The gains are shared between households in all parts of the income distribution except at the very top (where households are unlikely to qualify for main council tax benefit) but they are concentrated in deciles 3, 4 and 5. Workless couples and unemployed single adults would be the biggest gainers since they would no longer lose benefit due to living with working non-dependants. But this reform would also mean that non-poor individuals who moved into households headed by those on benefit would escape council tax liability.

4.6.   Reform 6: Restrict Council Tax Benefit to a Band B Bill

Cap entitlement to council tax benefit at the amount that would be paid if the householder lived in a band B property.

Since April 1998, the maximum council tax benefit entitlement has been capped at the band E bill for the relevant local authority. We consider extending the restriction to band B. This might be advanced as a way of saving money and mean that the benefit system did not give more help to those who chose to live in more valuable properties.

Results

Restricting benefit entitlement to that corresponding to a band B bill would reduce modelled council tax benefit expenditure by over 10 per cent and reduce the numbers entitled by 200,000, in some cases by 'floating' some people off benefit altogether.

Because of the means testing of council tax benefit, it is only those with low incomes who lose from this cut, leaving the net burden of council tax much more regressive, as shown in Figure 4.5. The fraction of

FIGURE 4.5

**Change in net burden across the income distribution
following restriction to band B**

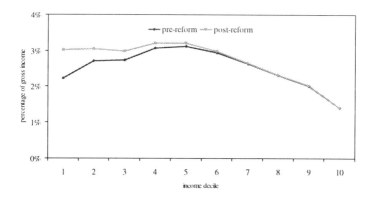

households in each decile that would lose more than £1 a week falls as we move up the income distribution. Overall, 1.3 million households actually claiming council tax benefit would lose more than £1 a week.

The biggest losers from this reform would be two groups that may face little realistic chance of living in properties classified as band A or B:

• Those living in the South-East and London where house prices are much higher, so many modest properties are allocated to higher-value bands. Twenty-three per cent of households in London would lose substantially.

• Poorer families with children, such as unwaged couples and lone parents. These groups typically require larger, and therefore more expensive, houses than the childless. Over 20 per cent of each of these groups would lose out by more than £1 a week.

4.7.   Reform 7: Pay Council Tax Benefit as if All Councils Spent at SSA

Pay council tax benefit at a fixed rate, irrespective of the actual tax bill set by each local council. Set this rate at the level payable if all councils spent at a centrally set level — the standard spending assessment.

Council tax benefit compensates households for the actual tax bill they face, providing more help to those who live in high-tax areas. Instead of benefit payments relating to actual council tax bills, they could relate to the council tax bill that a council would have set if it had set its budget at a centrally determined level, known as standard spending assessment (SSA). This reform might be advanced as a way to save money, as well as being a means to create a link between the council tax bills and net incomes of benefit recipients. But it would mean that council tax benefit no longer provided additional help to poorer families living in high-tax areas.

Results

Since almost all councils set a council tax rate above that implied by SSA, pegging council tax benefit at SSA would reduce benefit expenditure by about £570 million (a 17 per cent cut). But nationally uniform benefits would mean that poorer households in high-tax areas would slip below the safety net. The bottom two deciles can both expect average losses of over £1 a week. The top half of the income distribution is largely unffected because relatively few of their number are on benefit.

Figure 4.6 shows that the net burden of the tax increases sharply for the bottom decile, with smaller but still significant increases for the rest of the bottom half

FIGURE 4.6

Change in net burden across the income distribution resulting from council tax benefit being paid at level implied by SSA

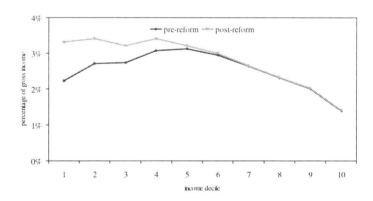

of the income distribution. This reform amounts to a cut in benefit similar in scale to that brought about by Reform 6. Although the two reforms affect different individual households, the overall effects across the income distribution are similar, leaving Figure 4.6 looking very similar to Figure 4.5.

Households in Scotland and northern England would tend to lose out from the reform, due to higher average council tax rates. Those in band A homes are the biggest losers, since they are more likely to be on benefit and are concentrated in less prosperous regions where council tax rates tend to be higher.

The introduction of nationally uniform benefits would ensure that all households faced a direct incentive, at the margin, to hold their local council to account for its budget decision. But, as with the community charge, councils would have to collect relatively small amounts of tax from low-income households, increasing administration costs and possibly causing greater compliance problems.

4.8.   Reform 8: Reduce Council Tax Bills

Reduce council tax bills by 20 per cent, the reduction being paid for by higher central grant. Leave the structure of council tax benefit unchanged.

None of the reforms to replace or modify council tax benefit that we have looked at has succeeded in solving all the problems of the existing system without introducing new difficulties or leading to higher expenditure. So an alternative strategy to reduce benefit expenditure without hitting vulnerable groups is to leave council tax benefit as it is but reduce the overall take of council tax. One reason for advancing this policy is that it might make reform of council tax benefit easier — the scale of the losses generated under almost all the major reforms that we have considered would be contained if reform were combined with lower council tax rates. We model a reduction in gross council tax bills of 20 per cent.

Results

The biggest obstacle to reducing council tax revenues by 20 per cent is the cost of £2.9 billion, although some £800 million could be claimed back in reduced benefit payments, giving a net cost of £2.1 billion. Nearly 400,000 people would be 'floated' off council tax benefit, a decrease of 5 per cent. Decreasing the numbers on means-tested benefits might have positive labour supply effects as it would reduce the numbers facing high effective marginal tax rates as a result of benefit withdrawal. The cut in council tax bills would also increase the financial attractiveness of moving into full-time work from benefits, as the resultant loss of full council tax benefit would become less significant.

Modelling suggests that poorer people would gain very little from cuts in council tax bills since many are entitled to benefit, which falls pound for pound with lower council tax bills. In practice, the non-take-up of benefit entitlement by many of those on low incomes would mean that many of the poor would gain. The biggest average cash gains are found amongst the richest households but the net council tax burden (as a percentage of income) would fall most for those in the middle of the income distribution, where the modelled burden was previously highest. Nearly all households that gain at all do so by more than £1 a week.

Two-earner couples stand to make the biggest average cash gains owing to their high average net council tax bills. But single-earner couples and (to a lesser extent) pensioner couples would make similar gains, and the lower average incomes of these families mean that the proportional effect on them would be greater.

4.9. Reform 9: Change Band Relativities

Change the 'band relativities' so that council tax liability increases more sharply across bands.

The council tax's regressivity with respect to income might be linked to its schedule with respect to property — bills represent a declining proportion of house price as property values increase. We model an alternative scheme that 'fans out' the existing band structure so that council tax liability increases more quickly as we move up the council tax bands. Table 4.1 shows how band relativities would change compared with the current system.

Results

The reform would cost £700 million in forgone council tax receipts, because far more people live in the low-band households, which now face lower bills, than live in the high-band homes, which face a rise. But most of

TABLE 4.1

Reform of council tax band relativities

Band	Old ratio to band D	New ratio to band D
A	12/18	9/18
B	14/18	12/18
C	16/18	15/18
D	1	1
E	22/18	24/18
F	26/18	30/18
G	30/18	36/18
H	36/18	45/18

FIGURE 4.7

**Change in net burden across council tax bands
following change in band relativities**

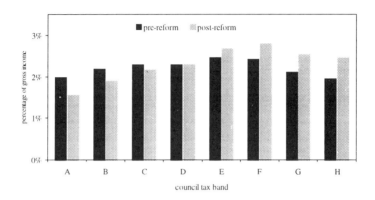

this loss — about £500 million — is 'reclaimed' through lower expenditure on council tax benefit for those living in low-value homes, leaving the net cost at £200 million. Falling bills in the lower bands also see around 250,000 people 'floated' off benefit altogether.

Figure 4.7 shows the change in the spread of the burden across the different bands. The average net burden is markedly lower in band A than previously, increasing more steeply through the bands than before, and tailing off less quickly for the highest-value homes. This stronger relation between council tax band and council tax liability would lead to increased pressure for revaluations as property prices change over time and a greater number of appeals against new evaluations, since the gain from being classified to a lower property band would be greater.

Changing band relativities would increase the progressivity of the tax with respect to income. The net burden rises for households in the top 10 per cent of the income distribution and is modelled to fall most in the middle of the income distribution. The bottom income decile is largely unaffected, as we are assuming 100 per cent take-up, so the near-universal benefit entitlement is seen to be exactly offsetting changes to council tax for households in this group. Under the more realistic assumption of imperfect take-up at the bottom of the income distribution, the poor families in low-banded properties who do not claim their benefit would gain.

Although it increases the system's progressivity, this reform could threaten the income safety net: poorer taxpayers who found it difficult to avoid living in expensive housing (being in high property-price regions or in large families) would be very hard hit. Within the bottom decile, the average loss amongst the small fraction (6 per cent) of households that lose more than £1 per week is large, at £2.39 a week. These households tend to be affected by council tax benefit entitlement being restricted to band E, so increases in tax liability for those in the highest-value properties are not matched by higher benefit payments. The creation of a small number of heavy losers amongst low-income families would be a concern, which might mean that any government considering this reform would also want to consider reversing the band E restriction. But this reform increases the level of bills for higher-banded homes, so it would also increase the cost of removing the band E restriction.

CHAPTER 5
Conclusions: The Policy Agenda

Reform of the Welfare State is central to the government's agenda, but it has so far paid little attention to reforming council tax benefit. In principle, the complex rules of the benefit effectively target the needy. But rising council tax bills have increased both the cost of the benefit and the numbers receiving it, and we have highlighted a number of problems with the way the system works. The system's great complexity helps explain the most important of these — low take-up, which threatens the income safety net. Reducing this complexity should produce fewer big losers than major reform of housing benefit, since council tax payments are typically much smaller than rents.

Outright abolition of council tax benefit combined with compensation through an increase in income support rates would represent a dramatic simplification of the benefit system, even when coupled with the minor reforms to other means-tested benefits it would necessitate. At a stroke, it would do away with all the complex rules of council tax benefit and reduce the number of benefits available to individuals.

None the less, we conclude that the outright abolition of local tax relief, when considered in isolation, has to be rejected if the notion of a national income safety net is to be taken seriously. The council tax bills facing low-income individuals are sufficiently high and sufficiently variable to ensure that attempting to compensate without use of a specific rebate would mean accepting significantly greater dispersion in the living standards of the poorest. More particularly, even if spending on other means-tested benefits were simultaneously significantly increased, some big losses for families at the bottom of the income distribution would have to be accepted. While it is true that many of those whom we model as losing from such a reform do not currently claim their benefit, abolition of this entitlement seems an unattractive way to deal with the genuine distributional problem of non-take-up.

The same reasoning leads us to reject reforms that would limit the extent to which council tax benefit payments vary with bills. The direct contribution of the council tax to the low incomes of many poor households means that withholding full compensation from some of them — by paying benefit at a flat rate across councils or by restricting maximum entitlement to the bills facing cheaper homes — would be to forgo an important method of targeting the needy. Besides, such schemes would bring little simplification.

Concern to protect the poorest must also rule out the more attractive of the local tax relief schemes from overseas that we examined — non-means-tested group exemptions. The failure to means test implies that any list of exemptions would result in either very many amongst the poorest being hard hit or a huge net exchequer cost, or, and most likely, both.

Taken in isolation, we do not see how solving council tax benefit's problems can be reconciled with the maintenance of the income safety net. But developments elsewhere in the tax and benefit system could increase the scope for change. Large increases in other means-tested benefits, to take them well above the level judged the acceptable minimum, are one possibility. We took the level of the safety net as being given by the rates of income support (and associated benefits) that applied in the social security system that we used as our base — that of April 1998. But the government has announced real increases in the minimum income awarded to pensioners, disabled people and families with children. If the increases are viewed as taking benefit levels above the safety net, then reform of local tax relief that leaves some income support recipients losing would cause less concern. If, instead, they are seen as increases in the acceptable minimum, then creating losses amongst these groups will continue to be judged unacceptable. Still, if the rates of these benefits were consistently increased, simplifying reform to council tax benefit would become more attractive.

But under current council tax rates, increases in other benefits would have to be very large to ensure that no one was left below the safety net. Cutting the tax's rates would attack the need for a specific benefit directly, and so facilitate reform. The lower level of local domestic property taxes in many other countries is surely one reason why the less targeted systems of relief found overseas are accepted. Likewise, the relatively small size of the highly regressive television licence helps to explain why it is accepted without a large-scale relief scheme. As well as making reform or abolition of council tax benefit easier, reversing recent increases in tax rates would help those low- and middle-income groups that currently face a high local tax burden because they do not receive any rebate.

If a combination of lower council tax rates and higher levels of means-tested benefits were ever to prevail, then the abolition of council tax benefit would become much more attractive, principally because of the simplification it would represent. But, in the short term, high (and upward-trended) tax rates mean that very steep increases in other means-tested benefits would be needed to ensure that the abolition of local tax relief did not throw many of those facing high bills into poverty.

APPENDIX A
The Council Tax Benefit System

A.1. Main Council Tax Benefit

The amount of benefit that a household is entitled to is worked out on the basis of three factors:

- the council tax bill that the claimant faces;
- the income that the claimant has (net of income tax and National Insurance and after adding in family credit); any savings are treated as giving rise to an imputed income;
- what the claimant needs to live on. This is called the *applicable amount* and is an amount of income set by the DSS. Its value depends on various features of the claimant, such as age, marital status and number of children.[32]

The three factors are related in the calculation by the following equation:

Benefit entitlement = Bill − 0.2 × (Income − Applicable amount).[33]

The last term (income minus applicable amount) is the income that the claimant has over and above the level that the DSS deems he or she needs. We call this *excess income*. For someone on income support, income is

---

[32]Its level is normally set at the income support rate that the claimant would receive had he or she no other income.

[33]The calculation is subject to two constraints. First, entitlement cannot be negative; for claimants for whom this calculation gives a negative number, entitlement is simply set to zero. Second, the value of the benefit has an upper bound of the total bill: benefit is set equal to bill even if income is less than the applicable amount.

equal to the applicable amount, so excess income is zero.

The calculation has a number of implications. First, the maximum entitlement to benefit is normally 100 per cent of the bill,[34] and this will be awarded to anyone with zero excess income. Second, for claimants with income that is greater than the applicable amount, entitlement will be reduced by 20p for every £1 of excess income possessed, until benefit entitlement is exhausted. This process is known as *tapering* and, as 20 per cent of excess income is forgone in reduced benefit entitlement, we say that the benefit has a taper of 20 per cent. Third, changes in council tax bills have no effect on the amount of net tax paid. For people on maximum benefit, this is obvious: if, for instance, such a recipient's council tax bill goes up, benefit entitlement continues to be set at 100 per cent of the bill so that there is no change in net income. The same holds for people in receipt of a partial rebate. In terms of the equation above, when the bill goes up, excess income is unchanged, so benefit changes to exactly offset the tax increase, leaving the cash amount of tax that the individual must pay unchanged.

A.2. Non-Dependant Deductions

Entitlement to main council tax benefit is reduced to reflect the income of other adults in the household, who are assumed to make a contribution towards meeting the bill. Non-dependant deductions apply when there are grown-up children who work but still live at home with

---

[34]Since the beginning of the last financial year (1998/99), this is no longer quite true: for new claimants with properties in bands F, G and H, maximum benefit is now calculated as the value that the bill would be if the house were in band E. Thereafter it is subject to tapering and non-dependant deductions in the normal way.

TABLE A.1

Rates of non-dependant deductions, 1998/99

Weekly income of non-dependant	Deduction
£250 or more	£6.00
£200–£249.99	£5.00
£116–£199.99	£4.00
Below £116	£2.00

low-income parents, or, indeed, elderly parents living with low-income children. The rates of non-dependant deductions depend on the income of these non-dependants. Means testing the income of non-dependent adults aggravates the standard problems of income assessment: claimants may find it hard to get, or be reluctant to attempt to get, information on the resources of their co-residents.

Table A.1 shows the weekly rates of non-dependant deductions.[35] Of the 638,000 council tax benefit recipients who live with non-dependants, just under half (288,000) incurred some deduction from their benefit as a result in May 1997.

A.3.   Second-Adult Rebates

This completely separate system of council tax benefit is related to the single-person discounts in council tax bills. It also applies to householders who live with an adult who is not directly liable for council tax. If the householder were to live alone, they would receive a 25

---

[35]Exemptions from non-dependant deductions are given to those on means-tested job-seekers' allowance and income support and to other adults, such as students and live-in carers, who are 'invisible' for council tax purposes. Lodgers, or others who pay rent, are exempt because the rent that they pay is part of the householder's income and so gives rise to tapering of benefit in the usual way. In recent years, the government has increased these benefit deductions in real terms from a maximum of £2 per week in 1993/94 to £6 per week in 1998/99.

TABLE A.2

Rates of second-adult rebate at various income levels, 1998/99

Income of second adult	Second-adult rebate as a percentage of council tax bill
On means-tested job-seekers' allowance or income support	25%
<£116	15%
£116–£151.99	7.5%
£152 or more	Nil

per cent discount. Second-adult rebate compensates them for the loss of this discount. If the second adult is on means-tested job-seekers' allowance or income support, the head of household is entitled to a 25 per cent discount regardless of his or her income. There are lower rates of discount available if the second adult has higher levels of weekly income, as shown in Table A.2. Second-adult rebates are not available if the second person pays rent under commercial agreement or if more than one person liable for the council tax lives in the dwelling. Only 45,000 householders claim this benefit.[36]

---

[36]Figure for February 1997 from *Social Security Statistics, 1997.*

APPENDIX B
Comparing the FRS Data with Administrative Data from the DSS

In Chapter 2, we argued that the Family Resources Survey estimates of average amount of council tax benefit and of the number of recipients of the benefit are very similar to the actual figures in DSS administrative statistics. Here, we compare statistics from the 1995/96 FRS with those from the 1995/96 edition of *Social Security Statistics* in more detail.

Figure B.1 shows numbers claiming different banded amounts of council tax benefit; both the figures from the FRS and those from the administrative statistics are shown. The FRS is close to administrative data not just with regard to the average amount received but also

FIGURE B.1

Distribution of council tax benefit recipients, by amount received: FRS and administrative statistics

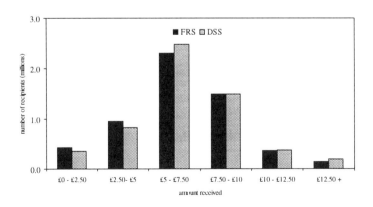

with its distribution. The only difference is that it tends to slightly overestimate low levels of receipt and slightly underestimate higher levels.

FIGURE B.2

**Distribution of council tax benefit recipients, by age:
FRS and administrative statistics**

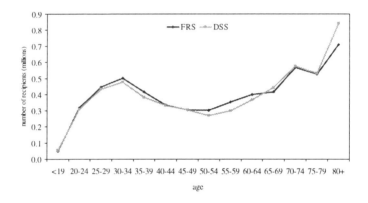

FIGURE B.3

**Distribution of council tax benefit recipients, by council tax band:
FRS and administrative statistics**

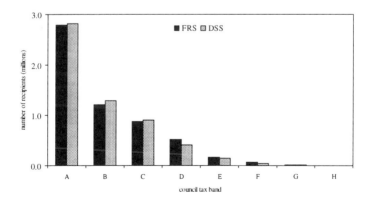

Another dimension where we can check against the administrative statistics is the age of recipients. Figure B.2 plots the distribution of recipients over a number of age brackets. Again, we see that the two numbers are very close, but that the FRS underestimates the number of the oldest pensioners who claim the benefit.

A final dimension in which the two sets of data can be readily compared is the council tax band of recipients. Figure B.3 again shows a close fit. The FRS slightly overestimates numbers in high bands relative to numbers in low bands.

References

Besley, T., Preston, I. and Ridge, M. (1997), 'Fiscal anarchy in the UK: modelling poll tax non-compliance', *Journal of Public Economics*, vol. 64, pp. 137–52.

Bryson, C. and Smith, N. (1996), *The Take Up of Second Adult Rebate*, Department of Social Security, Research Report no. 52, London: HMSO.

CIPFA (various years), *Finance and General Statistics*, London: Chartered Institute of Public Finance and Accountancy.

CIPFA Scotland (1995), *Rating Review, 1993–94*, Edinburgh:, Chartered Institute of Public Finance and Accountancy, Scottish Branch.

— (1996), *Rating Review, 1994–95*, Edinburgh: Chartered Institute of Public Finance and Accountancy, Scottish Branch.

Committee of the Regions (1996), *Regional and Local Government in the European Union*.

DETR (Department for the Environment, Transport and the Regions) (1998), *Improving Local Financial Accountability*, Consultation Document, London: DETR.

DoE (Department of the Environment) (1986), *Paying for Local Government*, Cmnd 9714, London: HMSO.

DSS (Department of Social Security) (1997), *Income Related Benefits: Estimates of Take Up in 1995/6*, Leeds: Corporate Document Services.

Giles, C., Johnson, P., McCrae, J. and Taylor, J. (1996), *Living with the State: The Incomes and Work Incentives of Tenants in the Social Rented Sector*, London: Institute for Fiscal Studies.

— and McCrae, J. (1995), 'TAXBEN: the IFS microsimulation tax and benefit model', Institute for Fiscal Studies, Working Paper no. 95/19.

— and Ridge, M. (1993), *Right This Time? An Analysis of the First Year's Council Tax Bills*, Commentary no. 37, London: Institute for Fiscal Studies.

McClements, D. (1977), 'Equivalence scales for children', *Journal of Public Economics*, vol. 8, pp. 191–210.

Raimondo, H. (1992), *Economics of State and Local Government*, New York: Praeger Publishers.

Does council tax benefit work?

Shaw, A., Walker, R., Ashworthy, K., Jenkins, S. and Middleton, S. (1996), *Moving Off Income Support: Barriers and Bridges*, Department of Social Security, Research Report.